OPPOSING
VIEWPOINTS®
SERIES

Euthanasia

Other Books of Related Interest:

Opposing Viewpoints Series

Abortion

Birth Defects

Ethics

Gendercide

At Issue Series

The Affordable Care Act

Extending the Human Lifespan

Medical Malpractice

The Right to Die

Current Controversies Series

Abortion

Death Penalty

Medical Ethics

Politics and Religion

"Congress shall make no law ... abridging the freedom of speech, or of the press."

First Amendment to the US Constitution

The basic foundation of our democracy is the First Amendment guarantee of freedom of expression. The Opposing Viewpoints series is dedicated to the concept of this basic freedom and the idea that it is more important to practice it than to enshrine it.

OPPOSING
VIEWPOINTS®
SERIES

Euthanasia

Margaret Haerens, Book Editor

GREENHAVEN PRESS
A part of Gale, Cengage Learning

GALE
CENGAGE Learning

Farmington Hills, Mich • San Francisco • New York • Waterville, Maine
Meriden, Conn • Mason, Ohio • Chicago

Patricia Coryell, *Vice President & Publisher, New Products & GVRL*
Douglas Dentino, *Manager, New Products*
Judy Galens, *Acquisitions Editor*

For more information, contact:
Greenhaven Press
27500 Drake Rd.
Farmington Hills, MI 48331-3535
Or you can visit our Internet site at gale.cengage.com

Articles in Greenhaven Press anthologies are often edited for length to meet page requirements. In addition, original titles of these works are changed to clearly present the main thesis and to explicitly indicate the author's opinion. Every effort is made to ensure that Greenhaven Press accurately reflects the original intent of the authors. Every effort has been made to trace the owners of copyrighted material.

Cover Image copyright © Phanie/Alamy.

LIBRARY OF CONGRESS CATALOGING-IN-PUBLICATION DATA

Euthanasia / Margaret Haerens, book editor.
  pages cm. -- (Opposing viewpoints)
Summary: "Opposing Viewpoints is the leading source for libraries and classrooms in need of current-issue materials. The viewpoints are selected from a wide range of highly respected sources and publications"-- Provided by publisher.
  Includes bibliographical references and index.
  ISBN 978-0-7377-7262-3 (hardback) -- ISBN 978-0-7377-7263-0 (paperback)
  1. Euthanasia. I. Haerens, Margaret, editor.
  R726.E77518 2015
  179.7--dc23
                                            2014030222

Printed in the United States of America
1 2 3 4 5 6 7 19 18 17 16 15

Contents

Chapter 3: What Controversies Impact the Euthanasia Debate?

Chapter 4: How Does the Affordable Care Act Affect the Euthanasia Debate?

Why Consider Opposing Viewpoints?

> *"The only way in which a human being can make some approach to knowing the whole of a subject is by hearing what can be said about it by persons of every variety of opinion and studying all modes in which it can be looked at by every character of mind. No wise man ever acquired his wisdom in any mode but this."*
>
> *John Stuart Mill*

In our media-intensive culture it is not difficult to find differing opinions. Thousands of newspapers and magazines and dozens of radio and television talk shows resound with differing points of view. The difficulty lies in deciding which opinion to agree with and which "experts" seem the most credible. The more inundated we become with differing opinions and claims, the more essential it is to hone critical reading and thinking skills to evaluate these ideas. Opposing Viewpoints books address this problem directly by presenting stimulating debates that can be used to enhance and teach these skills. The varied opinions contained in each book examine many different aspects of a single issue. While examining these conveniently edited opposing views, readers can develop critical thinking skills such as the ability to compare and contrast authors' credibility, facts, argumentation styles, use of persuasive techniques, and other stylistic tools. In short, the Opposing Viewpoints Series is an ideal way to attain the higher-level thinking and reading skills so essential in a culture of diverse and contradictory opinions.

In addition to providing a tool for critical thinking, Opposing Viewpoints books challenge readers to question their own strongly held opinions and assumptions. Most people form their opinions on the basis of upbringing, peer pressure, and personal, cultural, or professional bias. By reading carefully balanced opposing views, readers must directly confront new ideas as well as the opinions of those with whom they disagree. This is not to argue simplistically that everyone who reads opposing views will—or should—change his or her opinion. Instead, the series enhances readers' understanding of their own views by encouraging confrontation with opposing ideas. Careful examination of others' views can lead to the readers' understanding of the logical inconsistencies in their own opinions, perspective on why they hold an opinion, and the consideration of the possibility that their opinion requires further evaluation.

Evaluating Other Opinions

To ensure that this type of examination occurs, Opposing Viewpoints books present all types of opinions. Prominent spokespeople on different sides of each issue as well as well-known professionals from many disciplines challenge the reader. An additional goal of the series is to provide a forum for other, less known, or even unpopular viewpoints. The opinion of an ordinary person who has had to make the decision to cut off life support from a terminally ill relative, for example, may be just as valuable and provide just as much insight as a medical ethicist's professional opinion. The editors have two additional purposes in including these less known views. One, the editors encourage readers to respect others' opinions—even when not enhanced by professional credibility. It is only by reading or listening to and objectively evaluating others' ideas that one can determine whether they are worthy of consideration. Two, the inclusion of such viewpoints encourages the important critical thinking skill of objectively evaluating an author's credentials and bias. This evaluation will illuminate an author's reasons for taking a particular stance on an issue and will aid in readers' evaluation of the author's ideas.

It is our hope that these books will give readers a deeper understanding of the issues debated and an appreciation of the complexity of even seemingly simple issues when good and honest people disagree. This awareness is particularly important in a democratic society such as ours in which people enter into public debate to determine the common good. Those with whom one disagrees should not be regarded as enemies but rather as people whose views deserve careful examination and may shed light on one's own.

Thomas Jefferson once said that "difference of opinion leads to inquiry, and inquiry to truth." Jefferson, a broadly educated man, argued that "if a nation expects to be ignorant and free . . . it expects what never was and never will be." As individuals and as a nation, it is imperative that we consider the opinions of others and examine them with skill and discernment. The Opposing Viewpoints series is intended to help readers achieve this goal.

David L. Bender and Bruno Leone,
Founders

Introduction

Introduction

The controversy over euthanasia can be traced back to ancient times. Historical evidence suggests that a number of ancient cultures tolerated assisted suicide and euthanasia. For example, many ancient Greeks and Romans drank lethal poison to end their lives when faced with debilitating injury, life-limiting illness, or unbearable pain. In ancient Rome, suicide and assisted suicide were not only tolerated for those with terrible pain and illness, but also were widely accepted when an individual faced scandal or defeat at the hands of a political enemy. In some Greek city-states, suicide was a fairly common way to end one's life; in these regions, the poison used in suicides and assisted suicides was provided by the city magistrates. During this era, ancient Greeks also came up with a name for the practice: euthanasia, which means "a good death."

However, there was always opposition to euthanasia, even in these ancient cultures. The ancient Greek philosopher Aristotle deemed it to be a cowardly death and an offense against the state. Hippocrates, a prominent physician at the time, spoke explicitly against the practice in his Hippocratic Oath, which is still used by physicians all over the world today. "I will give no deadly medicine to any one if asked, nor suggest any such counsel," he vowed. Generation after generation of doctors took the oath and vowed to "do no harm" to their patients. Opposition to euthanasia hardened in the medical community—even if individual practitioners supported it under certain circumstances.

The spread of Christianity and Islam in the following centuries reinforced opposition to euthanasia. Both religious traditions prohibited the practice on moral grounds, deeming life to be sacred and suicide to be forbidden. In a number of religious traditions, physicians were explicitly prohibited from having a role in taking any life. Suffering was viewed as the wages of sin and a way for the individual to atone for wrongdoings.

Despite official religious condemnation of the practice, evidence exists that euthanasia was practiced, and even tolerated to some degree, in many communities on an individual level. The widespread death and suffering caused by the bubonic plague and other horrible disease led some philosophers and theologians to justify euthanasia in some circumstances and to rethink how society confronted dying.

By mid-nineteenth century, advances in medical understanding and technology spurred a further reassessment of euthanasia. Morphine and chloroform were being used for pain management for dying patients, and medical ethicists began to advance the idea that using these drugs to euthanize terminally ill patients was permissible because it ended the extreme suffering of the dying.

In the United States, a euthanasia movement emerged in the late nineteenth century, coinciding with the development of the modern hospital system. Felix Adler, a prominent activist and educator, was the first American to argue that patients suffering from chronic illness and unbearable pain had the right to commit suicide; moreover, he regarded it as ethical for physicians to play a role in such patients' deaths.

Legislation to legalize euthanasia was introduced in the state legislatures of Ohio and Iowa in 1906, but both measures eventually failed after contentious debates over the scope and morality of the proposed legislation. A similar movement in Great Britain in the 1930s also failed.

The euthanasia movement in the United States began to gather steam again in the 1970s with the emergence of the death with dignity movement. In 1980 a British American journalist, Derek Humphry, founded the Hemlock Society to provide information on suicide and assisted dying to the terminally ill. Humphry had become an advocate of voluntary euthanasia when his wife, Jean, was dying a prolonged, painful death from terminal cancer. The society also supported legislation to permit physician-assisted suicide in some situations. In 1992 Humphry published *Final Exit: The Practicalities of Self-Deliverance and Assisted Suicide for the Dying*, a manual for the terminally ill to commit suicide. The book was a huge success and proved to be very influential in the debate over euthanasia and the right to die movement.

The worldwide controversy surrounding the actions of physician Jack Kevorkian spurred further debate on the issue of physician-assisted suicide. By the late 1980s, Kevorkian had become a vocal advocate for the practice of assisted death, publishing several articles in American medical journals on the subject. He created a suicide machine that would allow a patient to simply press a button to have the machine administer a fatal dose of poison to end his or her life. In 1990 Kevorkian helped Janet Elaine Adkins, a fifty-four-year-old woman suffering from Alzheimer's disease, commit suicide with his machine.

Kevorkian went on to assist in the deaths of 130 people. In 1998 he was arrested after airing a tape on national television that showed him, for the first time, administering the lethal dose of poison himself to a patient in the final stages of amyotrophic lateral sclerosis (ALS), also known as Lou Gehrig's disease. Kevorkian was arrested, charged with second-degree murder, and convicted and sentenced to ten to twenty-five years in prison for the crime. He was paroled in 2007 for good behavior, and he died on June 3, 2011.

In 1994 Oregon voters passed an initiative to allow physician-assisted dying in limited circumstances. Known as the Oregon Death with Dignity Act, the law permits terminally ill patients to request in writing a dose of lethal medication to commit suicide with the help of a consenting physician. The law was not implemented until 1997 because of legal challenges, including a case heard by the US Supreme Court that allowed the law to stand.

In 2008 the state of Washington passed a similar initiative to permit physician-assisted dying under certain circumstances. Vermont became the third state to pass a death with dignity law in 2013, the first in New England and the first to pass through legislation. Although there is no state law on assisted dying in Montana, the state supreme court ruled that there was no state law prohibiting a physician from participating in an assisted suicide at a patient's request. In 2014 a court ruling in New Mexico said that terminally ill residents have a constitutional right to obtain a physician's aid in dying and that physicians who assist a patient in dying cannot be prosecuted under state law. The state's attorney general is appealing the ruling.

The authors of the viewpoints included in *Opposing Viewpoints: Euthanasia* explore the debate over the controversial practice in chapters titled "Should Governments Allow Euthanasia and Physician-Assisted Suicide?," "What Effect Does Euthanasia Have on Individuals and Society?," "What Controversies Impact the Euthanasia Debate?," and "How Does the Affordable Care Act Affect the Euthanasia Debate?" The information in this volume provides insight into the legal, political, and ethical issues that influence the debate on voluntary euthanasia and physician-assisted suicide.

CHAPTER 1

Should Governments Allow Euthanasia and Physician-Assisted Suicide?

Chapter Preface

Palliative care is often regarded as a better option than voluntary euthanasia and physician-assisted suicide for many people struggling with terminal illness and unbearable pain. Administered by a team of doctors, nurses, social workers, and other specialists in the field, palliative care works to improve the lives of patients by relieving pain and providing emotional support and comfort in what may be their final weeks or months. A vital component of palliative care is giving patients more control over their treatment by making sure they understand all medical options at every stage of the illness and alleviating pain to the point where patients can live their lives to the fullest for the time they have left.

In the United States, hospice care is a very popular form of palliative treatment. The number of Americans receiving hospice care grows every year. According to the National Hospice and Palliative Care Organization (NHPCO), around 1.6 million Americans were serviced by hospice programs in 2012. Hospice programs are usually reserved for patients with life-limiting illness. More than 90 percent of hospice programs are administered in a patient's home, but care is also provided in hospice centers, nursing homes, hospitals, and other long-term care facilities. Hospice care is available twenty-four hours a day, seven days a week.

The history of hospice in the United States can be traced back to an influential lecture given by the British physician Dame Cicely Saunders at Yale University in 1963. Saunders began to help the dying as a nurse in 1948 and over the years became a pioneer in the field of palliative medicine. She went on to train as a medical social worker and a physician, founding the first modern hospice, St. Christopher's Hospice, in London in 1967.

The lecture that Saunders gave at Yale is widely credited with starting the hospice movement in the United States. Speaking to a large group of medical students, social workers, nurses, and chaplains, she outlined her philosophy of hospice care: to alleviate pain and suffering; to preserve the dignity of patients in their final days of life; and to help dying patients confront the spiritual and psychological pain of death.

In 1969 a Swiss American psychiatrist, Elisabeth Kübler-Ross, published a seminal book entitled *On Death and Dying*. Based on Kübler-Ross's extensive experience working with dying patients, the international best seller identifies five states of grief that every individual confronts in the dying process: denial, anger, bargaining, depression, and acceptance. *On Death and Dying* also advocates for at-home hospice care instead of treatment in an institutional setting, arguing that dying patients should have more control over end-of-life decisions. The book's widespread popularity introduced the idea of hospice care to many Americans dealing with such situations with family members and spurred debate in many families about end-of-life planning.

The first hospice in the United States was established in 1974 in Branford, Connecticut. Funded by the National Cancer Institute (NCI), the hospice served as a model for future programs. By the late 1970s, the hospice movement was growing in the United States and gaining the support of the American medical establishment. Congress incorporated hospice care into Medicare coverage in the 1980s, and as part of veterans' benefit packages in 1991. Hospice care continued to grow over the years, and in 2005 the movement reached a milestone when the number of hospice providers surpassed four thousand.

Hospice care is still a growing field in the United States and is often cited as an alternative to voluntary euthanasia or physician-assisted suicide for end-of-life treatment. The debate between palliative care and euthanasia is examined in the following chapter, which considers whether governments should allow euthanasia and physician-assisted suicide to be legalized.

tion the first three times. However, he was convicted in 1997 for euthanizing a client whose illness, ALS, prevented him from taking his life. He not only took the client's life; he videotaped the event and it was telecast on a *60 Minutes* segment. It was used to convict him in the Michigan court.

Derek Humphry's wife died of cancer, in great, unmitigated pain at the end. He believed that such agony was cruel and unnecessary and advocated euthanasia to end the lives of dying patients. Toward that end, he founded the Hemlock Society, which provided persons with information to take a "final exit" from the pain of chronic illnesses such as cancer or ALS.

Why did these uncompromising men appear in the public eye at this time in history? Because American society was experiencing the "medicalization of death," a multifaceted event that began in the early decades of the 20th century. Death was given a medical character, as seen in enormous advances in medical technology, new inventions, and drugs. Hospitals were no longer places where poor people went to die; they had become places where sick people were treated and health restored. Doctors used these innovations to treat and cure their patients, even though extending their life led to unforeseen problems.

Medical science—with its new techniques and special departments (CPR, public health agencies, emergency departments, intensive care units, medical specialists) and its innovative lifesaving medicines and procedures (penicillin, organ and bone marrow transplants, artificial hearts and hips, defibrillators)—led to a near doubling of life expectancy. In 1900, the average life expectancy of an American was 47 years; in 2000, it was nearly 80 years.

In 1900, infectious diseases like tuberculosis and pneumonia were the primary causes of death. By 2000, degenerative diseases like cancer and heart disease were the major causes of death. Americans are living longer and dying more slowly of chronic diseases that rob them of a vibrant life and leave many of them in great pain, immobile, experiencing urinary and bowel incontinence, a loss of dignity, and totally dependent on others. This new medical reality has led to the PAD controversies.

The Choices a Terminally Ill Patient Confronts

Today a person facing a degenerative death has a limited number of choices available to address that grim reality. He can have lifesaving medical treatment withdrawn or withheld from his body. Under common and constitutional law, a competent person is an autonomous individual with the right to self-determination. He can make such a choice, even though it will lead to his death.

A second path—taken by growing numbers of terminally ill patients—is to treat the pain aggressively, even though it will hasten the patient's death. In 1974, there was a single hospice. By 2010, more than 40% of terminally ill people (a little more than one million persons) were aggressively treated for pain and suffering in hospice through palliative care.

These choices pose no legal or ethical problems. As long as the dying patient is competent, society's values allow such choices. Suicide is another path. It is no longer a criminal act in America, but many dying who contemplate this choice are put off because of the gross violence of a gunshot or a jump off a bridge. By 1990, there were groups of people—dying patients, death with dignity organizations, medical professionals—who called for a dignified way to die.

PAD is the final choice. It is today a criminal act in [47] states. If a doctor assists a dying patient by deliberately providing the knowledge, the means, or both, which the patient then uses to end his life, the physician is a criminal, subject to prosecution, loss of license, and imprisonment.

For some dying persons, the specter of a slow, painful, and humiliating period before biological death is too much. Their illness prevents them from leading the life they had before they contracted cancer or Parkinson's disease or ALS. They experienced social death and did not want to spend many months, in some cases years, awaiting biological death. They believe they have the constitutional liberty to take their life. Furthermore, they maintain that their doctor can assist them by providing information and prescribing the medications used to end their life.

Ethics

For PAD advocates, including this author, two principles are paramount in its defense: 1) patient liberty/autonomy, and 2) the doctor's duty to relieve suffering. The right to self-determination is guaranteed by the "liberty" provision in the U.S. Constitution's due process clause. A terminally ill patient has the liberty to choose death by receiving a fatal prescription from her doctor. It is an absolute right possessed by an individual; the government cannot abrogate it.

The second tenet is the compassionate medical practitioner who provides his dying, suffering, patient with a prescription that, if filled, will enable the patient to die with dignity. This medical procedure, PAD, is right; it is caring; it is moral.

Opposed to these arguments are conservative philosophers, scientists, clergy (especially the Roman Catholic hierarchy), doctors, nurses, politicians, lobbyists, and pressure groups. For all of them, there are limits to individual autonomy. And PAD is not a fundamental right. They believe that a more fundamental societal right—the sanctity of human life—trumps individual autonomy.

They categorically reject the second principle. The Hippocratic Oath's essential message, that doctors must "do no harm," is the primary guideline for doctors. Compassion is

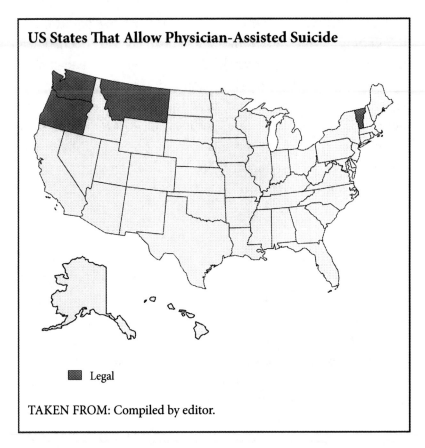

US States That Allow Physician-Assisted Suicide

■ Legal

TAKEN FROM: Compiled by editor.

not a substitute for appropriate medical treatment of the dying patient—until a patient refuses the treatment.

Law and Policy

The issue of PAD entered the courtrooms and legislative assemblies in 1990. In the courts, especially the U.S. Supreme Court, the essential question revolved around the scope of the Fourteenth Amendment's due process and equal protection clauses.

In 1990 every state had laws making assisting suicide a felony. PAD advocates in New York and Washington State went into federal courts to challenge them. Representing a small number of terminally ill patients (all dead by 1997), the lawyers presented two arguments in the trial and appellate courts. First, "liberty" in the due process clause is a fundamental right. Its scope extended to a terminally ill patient's liberty to die with dignity with the passive assistance of a medical practitioner.

Second, the state laws violated the "equal protection" clause of the 14th Amendment because they *allowed* the withdrawal of life support from a dying patient while *denying* another dying patient receiving a physician's assistance in dying. For the supporters of PAD, the two actions are not different: in both, death occurs.

Surprisingly, majorities in both appeals courts, the Second Circuit (New York) and the Ninth Circuit (Washington), accepted the arguments and invalidated the laws.

In *Washington v. Glucksberg*, 1997, the Supreme Court overturned the decision of the Ninth Circuit. Chief Justice [William] Rehnquist wrote the opinion for the court, focusing on the broad interpretation to "liberty."

The due process clause, he wrote, prevents substantial government interference with *fundamental* rights and liberties. Is PAD such a fundamental liberty? Was PAD "a deeply rooted" value in the nation's "history, legal traditions and practices." For Rehnquist, PAD was not such a value. Affirming the lower courts, he concluded, "would reverse centuries of legal doctrine and practice and strike down the considered policy choice of almost every state."

The court also overturned the Second Circuit. In *Vacco v. Quill*, Rehnquist concluded that New York's prohibition of PAD did not violate the 14th Amendment. PAD was not the equivalent of withdrawal from medical lifesaving procedures. In the former, taking the fatal dose of medication was the proximate cause of death. Refusing or withdrawing life-support procedures led to death; the underlying illness was the proximate cause of death. They are not the same; therefore, equal protection is not germane.

While the decisions were unanimous, 9–0, there were concurring opinions because of the technical issue the litigation raised. In both cases, all the patient-petitioners died. Consequently, the PAD lawyers had to present a "facial challenge" to the laws. This is a very tough standard to meet. The lawyers must show that there was *no set of circumstances* existing under which the law would be valid. If the patient-petitioners were alive in 1997, the lawyers would have presented an "as applied" challenge. In this scenario, they had to show that the law was invalid as applied to these patients. Concurring opinions strongly suggested the probability of validating the lower courts *had* the petitions been filed as "as-applied" challenges.

These two cases are precedent in American jurisprudence. There has been no new challenge to other state laws prohibiting physician assistance in dying. However, the battleground moved from the courtroom to legislative chambers and voting booths. Rehnquist's final message to the parties in both cases was prescient: "Our holding permits this debate to continue, as it should in a democracy." The debate did continue, in more than two dozen states.

In these legislative battles—and every one has been a bitter ideological fight—the pro-PAD advocates have fared poorly. Except for Oregon and Washington [and Vermont as of 2013], every proposed PAD bill was defeated. The major "anti" organizations remain the Roman Catholic Church, which has spent many millions of dollars to defeat the bills; professional organizations, especially the American Medical Association and nursing groups; organizations representing the physically disabled, such as the group Not Dead Yet; right-to-life political pressure groups, who view PAD battles as surrogate for the *Roe v. Wade* abortion clashes; and many Republican politicians—from state legislators to President George W. Bush.

PAD's Future

From the 1990 defeat of California's PAD/euthanasia proposal to the November 2012 defeat of the Massachusetts PAD bill, the "antis" have succeeded in blunting most efforts to pass PAD legislation. Only the voters in two northwestern states [and Vermont] and, in 2009, the Montana Supreme Court, and some federal judges have accepted the *rightness* of PAD.

Yet things are happening that suggest significant changes in society's attitudes about death and dying. We are finally confronting the reality of how we die. There was only one functioning hospice in 1974; there are now thousands of facilities in every state and territory. Palliative care was not part of medical school curricula; today it is an important specialization. As the baby boomers have to confront the tragedy of degenerative diseases that rob them of dignity, more of them have come to believe that PAD is the "least worst death."

Our society's history clearly shows how values evolve, how they become more inclusive. Times change, and the meaning of the Constitution's words has kept pace—slowly but surely—with these changes since 1789. For the past seventy years, there have been significant expansions of individual liberties. The privacy value has been expanded to protect marital, sexual, and abortion rights. I am sure that physician assistance in dying will eventually be seen as a constitutionally protected right that terminally ill patients can choose without hesitation. Compassion has been a major factor in the growth of individual rights in America. It is the major trigger in the PAD issue; it will ultimately generate acceptance of PAD as "the least worst death" for some human beings.

| *"With so many advances in palliative care and the treatment of pain, it really is quite unnecessary to argue for the legalised killing of patients, even if well intentioned."*

Euthanasia Should Not Be Legal

Bill Muehlenberg

Bill Muehlenberg is an ethicist, philosopher, author, blogger, and media commentator. In the following viewpoint, he suggests that the push for legalized euthanasia is misguided and immoral because it is an act that "directly and intentionally causes a person's death." In other words, he contends that euthanasia should be considered homicide. Muehlenberg points out that although many supporters of euthanasia want to cloud the issue, there is a big difference between deliberately ending a life and withholding care, which allows for a natural death. Intention is key in such ethical considerations, and euthanasia is a deliberate act of murder, he argues. Muehlenberg asserts that even if the push for legalized euthanasia is based on a sense of compassion, it is unconscionable for any civilized society to allow for the legalized killing of its own citizens.

As you read, consider the following questions:

1. What nation does Muehlenberg identify as headed down the path of legalized euthanasia?

2. According to ethicist Monique David, what do doctors become in circumstances of euthanasia and assisted suicide?

3. How does the author differentiate the administration of pain relief, which could hasten death, from assisted suicide?

With a Labor/Green government now in power [in Australia], the culture of death is being further emboldened to push its agenda. A number of states are pushing for legalised euthanasia and already the Greens' federal leader Bob Brown is telling us that our number one national priority must be the right to kill.

Indeed, people now speak about a "right to die" and many pro-euthanasia societies have sprung up, actively lobbying on behalf of their cause. The push for legalised euthanasia is on the increase, and some nations have already headed down that path, most notably the Netherlands.

This push is often done in the name of compassion. But it is a strange kind of compassion which says that the way to relieve suffering is to kill the sufferer. With so many advances in palliative care and the treatment of pain, it really is quite unnecessary to argue for the legalised killing of patients, even if well intentioned.

The case against legalised euthanasia needs to be spelled out in detail. I have done that in other articles, but sometimes we need to go back to basics. In order to think clearly about this issue, we must make sure our terminology is carefully and sharply defined.

Terminology

It needs to be pointed out from the outset that euthanasia is not about halting futile treatment. Nor is it about the alleviation of suffering (this is known as palliative care). Euthanasia is an act that directly and intentionally causes a person's death. As one ethicist states, there is a "crucial difference between taking a life intentionally and allowing a death naturally. The first is homicide, and the second is a natural death".

The distinction amounts to this: There is a huge difference between letting nature take its course and actively hastening or inducing a patient's death. Because this is such an important point, and one which is so often confused (often deliberately by the pro-euthanasia camp), it is worth spending a bit of time on this, quoting a number of authorities.

Ethicist Daniel Callahan offers this distinction between allowing to die and intentional killing: "A lethal injection will kill both a healthy person and a sick person. A physician's omitted treatment will have no effect on a healthy person. . . . It will only, in contrast, bring the life of a sick person to an end because of an underlying fatal disease. . . . The doctor who, at the patient's request, omits or terminates unwanted treatment does not kill at all. Her underlying disease, not his action, is the physical cause of the death."

As Andrew Lansdown explains, "euthanasia has little to do with refusing futile or extreme treatment. The man who rejects a heart transplant or declines a third bout of chemotherapy is not committing suicide, but rather is accepting the inevitability of his own death. The doctor who withholds or withdraws undue treatment at the request of a terminally ill patient is not killing his patient but rather is refusing to prolong his patient's life at any cost. Properly understood, euthanasia involves an intentional act to end a person's life. Opponents of euthanasia do not advocate the unnecessary and unwelcome prolonging of human life by artificial means. Rather, they oppose active measures to bring human life to a premature end."

Indeed, it needs to be repeated that the refusal of treatment is not to be confused with euthanasia. Both the cause and intent of death are quite different. As ethicist Margaret Somerville explains, "In refusals of treatment that result in death, the person dies from their underlying disease—a natural death. The withdrawal of treatment is the occasion on which death occurs, but not its cause. If the person had no fatal illness, they would not die. In contrast in euthanasia, the cause of death is the lethal injection. Without that, the person would not die at that time from that cause."

A Right to Be Killed

Monique David puts it this way: "Currently, there is much confusion; many accept euthanasia because they do not want their lives to be maintained artificially nor to become victims of excessive treatment. However, these practices can be legitimately refused by the patient or their family through the ethical perspective of the right to die within the limits of natural death. Euthanasia and assisted-suicide advocates claim something else: the right to terminate life at the moment and in the way that the individual chooses—or that someone chooses for them.

"Therefore, we should not use these terms to refer to the right to die (because this right is intrinsic), but rather to the right to be killed. This desire, expressed as a personal right, demands the intervention of a third party and a legal system that authorizes it. In other words, euthanasia and assisted suicide imply that doctors become agents of death and that society legally recognizes a criminal act to be lawful; or even more pernicious, a medical act."

As ethicist Leon Kass reminds us, the ambiguity of the term "right to die" blurs the "difference in content and inten-

What Is Euthanasia?

Euthanasia usually refers to the act of a physician or health provider who brings a patient's life to an end by directly administering a lethal medication with the purpose of relieving the patient's suffering. Euthanasia can also refer to deliberate acts of omission, such as withholding technology that sustains nourishment in a person unable to eat and drink, or that supports respiration in a person unable to breathe. Euthanasia can be voluntary, when it is performed upon a patient's explicit and direct request. Nonvoluntary euthanasia occurs when the patient is unconscious or incompetent and is thus unable to make a decision. Physician-assisted suicide occurs when a physician provides the means, guidance, and information that enable a patient to end his or her own life (often by prescribing a lethal dose of medication), but does not directly administer the drugs.

"Assisted Suicide and Euthanasia,"
Global Issues in Context Online Collection, 2014.

tion between the already well-established common-law right to refuse surgery or other unwanted medical treatments and hospitalization, and the newly alleged 'right to die.' The former permits the refusal of therapy, even a respirator, even if it means accepting an increased risk of death. The latter permits the refusal of therapy, such as renal dialysis or the feeding tube, so *that* death *will* occur. The former would seem to be more about choosing how to live while dying, the latter mainly about a choice *for death*."

Finally, George Pitcher also makes some important distinctions: "Doctors regularly discontinue futile treatment. But they don't do it in order to end a patient's life. They are simply recognizing that death cannot be prevented by treatment. We need to understand that end-of-life decisions, which are made every day by doctors, aren't the same as life-ending decisions."

The Principle of Double Effect

One further issue in terminology needs to be addressed. This has to do with pain relief and the hastening of death. It should be pointed out that some forms of pain relief may have the unintended consequence of hastening death. When a suffering patient receives an injection of morphine to relieve pain, this may contribute to the speeding up of death.

But when pain relievers are administered, normally the intention is to relieve pain, not hasten death. In ethics, this is known as the principle of double effect. The intent was to do good (relieve pain) while an unintended side effect may occur (the hastening of death). Intention, again, is an important part of this whole debate.

John and Paul Feinberg explain the principle: "We are obligated both to preserve life and to relieve pain. Sometimes it may be impossible to do both. If it is impossible to preserve the life of the terminally ill, we are not immoral if we do not. Of course, there is still the obligation to relieve pain and suffering. If we do what we can to relieve pain and in the process hasten death, there is still no moral blame, since we could not preserve life."

Margaret Somerville points out the differences between euthanasia and pain-relief treatment: "In both cases, there is an effort to relieve suffering. The difference is that the primary aim of euthanasia is to do so by inflicting death, whereas the primary aim of pain-relief treatment is simply to relieve pain—not to shorten life or cause death (although either might be a secondary effect)."

Euthanasia, then, is about one thing only: the killing of another person. The intent is to kill someone. It does not matter whether this is done with a gun or a lethal injection—the effect is the same. No civilised society can permit the legalised killing of its own citizens, even if done in the name of compassion.

> "Bringing the age-old practice of what used to be called 'mercy killing' into the open, and relabelling it 'assisted suicide' and dangerously extending its remit to cover not just the close-to-death but also the physically disabled and the depressed, would be very bad indeed."

Euthanasia Should Be Illegal but Tacitly Permitted

Brendan O'Neill

Brendan O'Neill is an author and editor at Spiked. *In the following viewpoint, he asserts that a compassionate society should turn a blind eye to the act of assisted death and euthanasia, but it should not sanction the practice by legalizing it. O'Neill argues that assisted death should be kept private, the result of decisions made between family, friends, doctors, and the patient. It would be dangerous to allow the process to become a public spectacle and discussed and regulated by public officials. Then the act becomes a state-sanctioned killing and not a private act of mercy for a beloved family member. O'Neill believes that legalizing euthanasia would be bad for society because it would devalue human life instead of appreciating and celebrating it.*

Brendan O'Neill, "Ray Gosling and Problem with Euthanasia," www.spiked-online.com, February 18, 2010. Copyright © 2010 spiked Ltd. All rights reserved. Reproduced with permission.

As you read, consider the following questions:

1. Who did British broadcaster Ray Gosling purport to euthanize, according to the viewpoint?

2. According to the author, what British public figure has drawn up a list of situations in which it would be acceptable to seek death?

3. What public figure does O'Neill identify as a proponent of suicide tribunals?

The case of Ray Gosling, the 70-year-old broadcaster who revealed on BBC TV's *Inside Out* that he killed his lover who was dying from AIDS, captures one of the key problems with the campaign to legalise assisted suicide. Not content with the fact that society has traditionally ignored such instances of assisted voluntary euthanasia, knowing that they take place but choosing not to make a fuss about them, Gosling seems to want society to go a step further and *sanction* such acts. He appears to want public approval for what he did.

But that is not something society should give. For while it is compassionate to turn a blind eye to the assisted deaths of those in terminal pain, it would be wrong—and it would set a dangerously misanthropic precedent—to give a social, cultural blessing to such deaths. Tacitly tolerating assisted deaths is a very different thing from celebrating them, and the problem with today's increasingly influential pro-euthanasia lobby is that it wants society to say 'Yes, it is okay to kill' rather than what it currently says: nothing.

The Gosling Case

In his piece to camera for the East Midlands TV show *Inside Out*, Gosling was vague about the facts of his alleged act. He didn't give the name of the person he claims to have killed or where and when the alleged killing took place. He said he was in a hospital with his lover, who was in the final stages of AIDS and who wanted to die, when he asked the doctor to leave them alone. He then apparently smothered his lover with a pillow until he was dead and told the doctor when he returned: 'He's gone.'

It is of course perfectly understandable, and acceptable, that the doctor, who seems to have known what took place, and the dead man's family, some of whom also knew, did not report Gosling to the authorities. Helping terminally ill people to die is as old as humanity itself. Not everybody does it as dramatically as Gosling claims he did—most of the time, a doctor administered too much morphine, or the son or daughter of an extremely ill person whispered to a nurse: 'Please put her out of her misery'—but for centuries, in the family home, in hospitals and in care homes, individuals have helped hopeless loved ones to die.

No one in their right mind would suggest sending the police to hospices around the country to investigate alleged mercy killings, and it is virtually unheard of for a medical professional to be arrested for 'assisting death'. We tacitly accept that the important rules governing life and death—where of course murder is a crime, as is helping an individual to commit suicide—do not always apply towards the very end of life, if a terribly ill person expresses a desire to die or a family asks a doctor to end a loved one's suffering.

But the problem arises when campaigners call upon society not only passively to accept that these acts of humanity take place, but actively to welcome them, to sanction them, even to celebrate them. Gosling and some of his supporters in the assisted suicide lobby say they want to bring these acts 'into the open', to raise awareness about them, and to encourage society to create new rules outlining when it is acceptable to help end someone's life. But such acts do not belong 'in the open'. If society were to legalise assisted suicide, it would send the very profound message that death is an acceptable solution to life's trials and traumas. At a social level, it would elevate hopelessness and fatalism above the cultural affirmation of living, loving, fighting for another day, week, month or year.

The Problem with Clarity

All of us can accept that, behind closed doors, families and doctors sometimes make the intensely difficult decision that an individual's situation has become hopeless. But none of us should welcome the public institutionalisation of hopelessness, the writing into law of the idea that it is sometimes okay to choose death rather than life. A good society's focus should be on the extension and improvement of human life, ensuring people have the means and resources to live as long, as healthily, as comfortably and as freely as possible. Such a society can also show compassion towards the extremely ill who want to die, but by turning away and allowing them to make their decisions, not by elevating their predicament into some kind of national standard of When Death Is Acceptable.

Campaigners for the legalisation of assisted suicide say the problem is that the law is fudged and we need more clarity, in order to give sick individuals the 'right to die' and to protect from punishment any loved ones who help them. In fact, sometimes a fudge *is* better than clarity. Bringing the age-old practice of what used to be called 'mercy killing' into the open, and relabelling it 'assisted suicide' and dangerously extending its remit to cover not just the close-to-death but also the physically disabled and the depressed, would be very bad indeed—both for people who want to die and people who want to live.

It would be bad for people who want to die because it would formalise and drag out what is by its very nature an intensely private, agonising and usually quite quick decision. Keir Starmer, the UK's director of public prosecutions, has drawn up a list of situations in which it would be acceptable to seek death; another suggestion is to have 'assisted suicide tribunals' at which the terminally ill could make their case for dying. Imagine a 92-year-old woman on the cusp of death who wants to be hurried along, or a 45-year-old man in the final days of terminal cancer who wants that extra shot of morphine, having to ask permission from a bunch of bureaucrats.

Keeping Private Decisions Private

Formalising mercy killings would turn a deeply private family decision into a public spectacle. Indeed, mercy killing would become virtually impossible in these circumstances, since the 'mercy' bit—the doctor-family decision to exercise their humanity towards someone in extreme suffering—would be replaced by the sanction of the state. These would become state-sanctioned killings, not acts of humanity. The humane thing to do is to leave acts of mercy killings in private—yes, *behind closed doors*—where they belong and where they can be carried out in a properly humane fashion.

Even more importantly, legalising assisted suicide would be bad for those who want to live, too, for those who may be extremely ill, very badly disabled or just plain old, yet who can still see the magic in life and who think pain is a price worth paying for continued existence. The formalisation of death as a solution to hardship hints at a society that devotes a great deal of its energy and resources, and certainly its most impassioned liberal campaigning, not to the improvement of human life but to the creation of exit strategies for sick, exhausted and very old people.

The Value of Human Life

Some of the more shrill critics of legalising assisted suicide argue that it will lead to 'death panels' at which our grannies will be forced to 'choose death'. It won't. But it would reveal a society that seems incapable of truly valuing human life, especially elderly human life, in its profoundness and complexity. When author Terry Pratchett, who suffers from early-onset Alzheimer's [disease], suggested creating assisted suicide tribunals, he was championed by numerous commentators, one of whom described the rising numbers of old people with mental health issues as a 'social catastrophe' and pointed out that each patient with dementia costs the economy 'eight times as much as someone with heart disease'. Is this how we measure human life today? By its financial implications? The rush to legalise assisted suicide speaks to a society that has given up on celebrating human life in favour of thinking up ways to help people die.

'Nothing human is alien to me.' And sometimes, the desire to die, when in terminal decline, is a very human thing. But what is alien to me is a society that celebrates this very occasional desire to die, a society which is so down on life, so incapable of recognising that there is more to being human than the bodily and the bovine, so devoid of any vision for including elderly people in particular in the social makeup, that it instinctively, inexorably, almost thoughtlessly exerts more energy thinking up ways for people to leave this mortal coil than ways to improve existence upon it.

> "Respect for the intrinsic value of life provides a motivation to alleviate pain at the end of life. And a commitment to improving palliative care might eradicate demand for assisted suicide."

Palliative Care Is a Better Option for the Terminally Ill than Euthanasia

Adam J. MacLeod

Adam J. MacLeod is a legal analyst and commentator, law professor at Faulkner University, and visiting fellow at the James Madison Program in American Ideals and Institutions at Princeton University. In the following viewpoint, he finds that palliative care is a better option than euthanasia for terminally ill patients because palliative care expresses a respect for life that euthanasia and assisted suicide do not. Such a distinction is morally important, MacLeod argues, because those involved in a patient's care—especially the physician—should all be oriented toward life and not death. MacLeod contends that if palliative care hastens death, it is morally acceptable because the patient's death is a foreseen consequence, but not the intended conse-

quence. MacLeod states that the intention of physicians and medical professionals should be to relieve pain and comfort the dying, not end patients' lives.

As you read, consider the following questions:

1. What medical group does the author identify as recently voting to affirm its opposition to physician-assisted suicide?

2. Why does the author consider the choice between suicide and suffering as a false one?

3. According to MacLeod, in what state is palliative care declining?

The Massachusetts Medical Society recently voted to affirm its opposition to physician-assisted suicide. This vote matters because a movement is now afoot to decriminalize assisted suicide in Massachusetts (and elsewhere). If successful, this movement would enlist physicians to assist in acts of self-murder. The physicians want no part in that. The president of the Massachusetts Medical Society, Lynda Young, stated, "Physicians of our Society have clearly declared that physician-assisted suicide is inconsistent with the physician's role as healer and health care provider." Aiding the deliberate destruction of human life has no place in the doctor's job description.

Equally important is the society's affirmation of its commitment to palliative care. The policy, according to Young, expresses "support for patient dignity and the alleviation of pain and suffering at the end of life," and encourages physicians "to contribute to the comfort and dignity of the patient and the patient's family." As the society acknowledges, palliation is an important part of the doctor's vocation. Doctors rightly provide comfort to the dying, even when they know that death inevitably approaches. Unlike assisted suicide, palliative care is not inconsistent with the physician's commitment to life and health.

The Role of Palliative Care

Physicians in Massachusetts thus grasp a fundamental distinction that proponents of assisted suicide elide. That is the difference between choosing to cause death and choosing instead to provide comfort, knowing, but not intending, that death might be hastened as a result.

Proponents of assisted suicide obscure this distinction by focusing exclusively on consequences and ignoring purpose and intent. They observe that a terminally ill patient, who qualifies for physician-assisted suicide in those states that now allow it, is going to die no matter what. Why should it matter whether that death comes about as a result of a deliberate act or rather in the natural progression of the disease? Indeed, they insist, it is uncaring not to help the patient kill himself, to leave the patient exposed to the pains of a debilitating illness.

The choice between suicide and suffering is a false choice. Physicians do and should act with a purpose to relieve pain. Palliative care expresses respect for the lives of suffering patients, including those patients who are about to die. To acknowledge that death is inevitable is not to choose death; the fact that death occurs is not itself morally significant. But whether we choose death or not *is* morally significant.

Intention

A physician who helps her terminally ill patient live out his last days with as little pain as possible, even if this means hastening death, has not failed morally. Her action is every bit as reasonable as an act of self-defense, prosecution of a just war, or any other act that results in death, where the death is a

What Is Palliative Care?

Palliative care

- provides relief from pain and other distressing symptoms;

- affirms life and regards dying as a normal process;

- intends neither to hasten or postpone death;

- integrates the psychological and spiritual aspects of patient care;

- offers a support system to help patients live as actively as possible until death;

- offers a support system to help the family cope during the patient's illness and in their own bereavement;

- uses a team approach to address the needs of patients and their families, including bereavement counselling, if indicated;

- will enhance quality of life, and may also positively influence the course of illness;

- is applicable early in the course of illness, in conjunction with other therapies that are intended to prolong life, such as chemotherapy or radiation therapy, and includes those investigations needed to better understand and manage distressing clinical complications.

"WHO Definition of Palliative Care,"
World Health Organization, 2014.

foreseen consequence but is not intended. In other words, the principle of double effect applies to health care providers, just as it applies to everyone else.

By contrast, one's *purpose* with respect to death is extremely important. It is the choosing of death, acting with a purpose that death will result, that is morally problematic. Death is not something to be chosen, least of all by doctors. A physician who adopts the death of her patient as the purpose for her action has become a different kind of physician. Indeed, she has become a different kind of person. She has become a person who chooses death over life.

A person who purposely chooses to cause death, who makes death a reason for his actions, is not oriented toward the good. This is because choosing has a creative, self-making significance. To adopt by free choice a reason for one's action is to make that reason part of one's projects and commitments. By choosing life, one becomes a person oriented toward life. By choosing death, one becomes a person oriented toward death.

Life or Death

A person who is oriented toward life is going to act very differently than a person who is oriented toward death. Once one has adopted death as his purpose, death becomes a potential reason for action in later instances. One who considers purposeful death as an option will consider it reasonable to weigh the deliberate destruction of life against more costly alternatives, such as extended palliative care. If death itself is a reason for action, then nearly any hardship in life is sufficient to justify death. Addressing the underlying cause of the hardship is viewed as merely one option, and self-murder is often a less costly alternative.

For these reasons, the availability of assisted suicide is the enemy of palliative care. Perhaps this is why some have found that palliative care is declining in Oregon, where physician-assisted suicide has been permitted for several years. Indeed, there is good reason to believe that opposition to assisted suicide and concern about patient suffering, far from being enemies, actually go hand in hand. Respect for the intrinsic value of life provides a motivation to alleviate pain at the end of life. And a commitment to improving palliative care might eradicate demand for assisted suicide.

Human beings have value simply by virtue of their being alive. This does not mean that the value of life is absolute, that measures should always be taken to prolong life, or that one should never take any action that might hasten death. But we should not ask physicians to act with a purpose to bring about the death of their patients. We could not so alter the role and character of physicians without causing serious harm to their profession and to those whom they serve.

"The issues on the table are too important for hysterical indignation and fundamental religious dogma."

Euthanasia: Hope You Never Need It, but Be Glad the Option Is There

Philip Nitschke

Philip Nitschke is an author, pro-euthanasia activist, and the director of Exit International. In the following viewpoint, he underscores the need for a calm, mature, and intelligent discussion of euthanasia and the difficult issues associated with the practice. Nitschke points to several recent controversies in Belgium surrounding legislation to extend the right to euthanasia to those who have Alzheimer's disease and to terminally ill children, both of which have inspired stiff opposition and public outrage all over the world. He urges people to have a respectful debate on the issues, without resorting to the moral panic and "hysterical indignation" that some elements of society will inevitably exhibit. Nitschke argues that these issues deserve a measured approach and consideration of what is best for those impacted by the debate.

As you read, consider the following questions:

1. According to the author, where was the world's first right to die law passed?

2. What New Zealand politician proposed a bill to allow assisted suicide to be written into living wills?

3. What country does the author identify as worthy of applause for its compassionate and evolved debate on euthanasia and assisted suicide?

The time was always going to come when society would need to face the pointy end of the voluntary euthanasia debate: Those hard cases that would challenge most people's support for the issue, the cases and circumstances which constitute never-before trodden ground.

While in most Western countries polls repeatedly show strong community support for a terminally ill person's right to obtain medical assistance to die, the results would likely be quite different if the person involved was not an adult, was not of sound mind or was not, in the strictest sense, terminally ill.

As Belgium decides whether to extend the right to euthanasia to those who have Alzheimer's [disease] and to children, the sharp end of the debate is staring us all in the face, regardless of where we live.

A Growing Debate

The euthanasia argument is about to escalate to heights unknown: We will all be challenged about how to have a good debate, a rational debate as members of the human race, and in being challenged, we must guard against the moral panic that this issue will inevitably throw up.

The issues on the table are too important for hysterical indignation and fundamental religious dogma. We are all grown-

Key Facts About Dementia and Alzheimer's Disease

- Dementia is a syndrome in which there is deterioration in memory, thinking, behaviour and the ability to perform everyday activities.

- Although dementia mainly affects older people, it is not a normal part of ageing.

- Worldwide, 35.6 million people have dementia and there are 7.7 million new cases every year.

- Alzheimer's disease is the most common cause of dementia and may contribute to 60–70% of cases.

- Dementia is one of the major causes of disability and dependency among older people worldwide.

- Dementia has a physical, psychological, social and economical impact on caregivers, families and society.

"Dementia: Key Facts,"
World Health Organization, April 2012.

ups. The debate we are set to have—some two decades after the world's first right to die law was passed in Australia's Northern Territory—should be grown-up too, even if some of the stakeholders we are about to discuss are not.

Historically, children and people with Alzheimer's are two segments of the community that have been viewed as having little or no agency, something that is referred to as 'capacity' in legal terms. Generally speaking, neither group has been held to be competent to make decisions that would be in their best interests. Yet this is what the Belgians are now planning.

Planning and Preparation

For many in the ageing population, there are few fears which top that of getting dementia. Anyone who has watched a loved family member sink into the abyss of confusion and disorientation will know the utter terror that can accompany the process, as the person in question tries to juxtapose moments of clarity with the awfulness of knowing one's grip on reality—and with it one's dignity and sense of self—is slipping.

In New Zealand earlier this year [2013], the Labour member of Parliament Maryan Street paved the way with her private members bill which, if passed, would allow New Zealanders to include an assisted suicide in their living will.

For those who may find themselves with Alzheimer's in the future, this inclusion would be a valuable pre-planning tool: "If I do get dementia, at least the children will know what I want. I can now rest assured that my wishes not to live 'like that' will be respected."

Within the membership of Exit International, this is a common sentiment. So too is the wish not to waste government money keeping the demented elderly alive in the nation's care homes if that is not how, when they could communicate, they said they wanted to spend their last days.

Tough Decisions

On the topic of children, the debate is a little easier. Some children do develop terminal illnesses and do die well before their time. It is not impossible for such young people to have a well-developed sense of their own mortality.

While the Belgians will likely structure legislative developments in this area with stringent safeguards, it is the practice of forcing terminally ill children to battle on in spite of an appalling prognosis, trying to make it to 18, that is driving the agenda.

For both groups, the Belgians are bravely tackling difficulties emerging in their existing legislation, current laws that are quite obviously inadequate, even cruel, in certain circumstances.

Unless modern medicine has a cure for Alzheimer's and any number of the terminal illnesses that confront children, the current situation is that they will keep suffering.

If suffering cannot be relieved, the question then becomes: What should the state do? Should we all be forced to live on regardless of the quality of life that confronts us? Or, should legislation be extended to ensure dignity and choice for all?

At Exit International, our motto is "a peaceful death is everybody's right." Somehow the tagline "a peaceful death is everybody's right unless you are a child or a teenager or have dementia, in which case tough luck!" doesn't have the same appeal or the same logic.

The Belgians are to be applauded for their progressive thinking and acting—in the cold light of day, the morality of their intentions is not that challenging when the alternatives are considered.

As a son to my aged mother and as a grandfather to my son's three boys, I welcome the type of society that the Belgians are proposing. Of course, I hope no one I love will ever need to use such laws. But I draw great comfort from knowing they are there all the same.

> *"Why, when it comes to dying, do demo-*
> *cratic institutions so often fail to trans-*
> *late what people want into legislation?"*

There Is a Right to Die

Peter Singer

Peter Singer is an influential thinker, author, and professor of bioethics at Princeton University as well as a professor laureate at the University of Melbourne. In the following viewpoint, he reviews the findings of a 2011 Royal Society of Canada report that examines end-of-life decisions from a bioethical perspective. The report concludes that terminally ill patients have the right of individual autonomy and self-determination, and therefore have the right to determine the means of their own deaths. Singer concurs with the report's findings, believing that individuals should have the right to end their lives on their own terms. Much of the opposition to this idea, he finds, originates with religious institutions, which have been very successful in stifling legislation despite strong public support.

As you read, consider the following questions:

1. Who does Singer identify as the chair of the expert panel of the Royal Society of Canada that was responsible for the report in 2011 on decision making at the end of life?

2. According to the report, what percentage of deaths did euthanasia account for in the Netherlands in 2005?

3. According to the report, what percentage of deaths did euthanasia account for in Belgium in 2007?

Dudley Clendinen, a writer and journalist, has amyotrophic lateral sclerosis (ALS), a terminal degenerative illness. In the *New York Times* earlier this year [2011], he wrote movingly both of his current enjoyment of his life, and of his plan to end it when, as he put it, "the music stops—when I can't tie my bow tie, tell a funny story, walk my dog, talk with Whitney, kiss someone special, or tap out lines like this."

A friend told Clendinen that he needed to buy a gun. In the United States, you can buy a gun and put a bullet through your brain without breaking any laws. But if you are a law-abiding person who is already too ill to buy a gun, or to use one, or if shooting yourself doesn't strike you as a peaceful and dignified way to end your life, or if you just don't want to leave a mess for others to clean up, what are you to do? You can't ask someone else to shoot you, and, in most countries, if you tell your doctor that you have had enough, and that you would like his or her assistance in dying, you are asking your doctor to commit a crime.

The Right to Self-Determination

Last month, an expert panel of the Royal Society of Canada, chaired by Udo Schüklenk, a professor of bioethics at Queen's University, released a report on decision making at the end of life. The report provides a strong argument for allowing doctors to help their patients to die, provided that the patients are competent and freely request such assistance.

The ethical basis of the panel's argument is not so much the avoidance of unnecessary suffering in terminally ill patients, but rather the core value of individual autonomy or self-determination. "The manner of our dying," the panel concludes, "reflects our sense of what is important just as much as do the other central decisions in our lives." In a state that protects individual rights, therefore, deciding how to die ought to be recognized as such a right.

The report also offers an up-to-date review of how assistance by physicians in ending life is working in the "living laboratories"—the jurisdictions where it is legal. In Switzerland, as well as in the US states of Oregon, Washington, and Montana [as well as Vermont as of 2013], the law now permits physicians, on request, to supply a terminally ill patient with a prescription for a drug that will bring about a peaceful death. In the Netherlands, Belgium, and Luxembourg, doctors have the additional option of responding to the patient's request by giving the patient a lethal injection.

The Survey Results

The panel examined reports from each of these jurisdictions, with the exception of Montana (where legalization of assistance in dying occurred only in 2009, and reliable data are not yet available). In the Netherlands, voluntary euthanasia accounted for 1.7% of all deaths in 2005—exactly the same level as in 1990. Moreover, the frequency of ending a patient's life *without* an explicit request from the patient fell by half during the same period, from 0.8% to 0.4%.

Indeed, several surveys suggest that ending a patient's life without an explicit request is much *more* common in other countries, where patients cannot lawfully ask a doctor to end their lives. In Belgium, although voluntary euthanasia rose from 1.1% of all deaths in 1998 to 1.9% in 2007, the frequency of ending a patient's life without an explicit request fell from 3.2% to 1.8%. In Oregon, where the Death with Dignity Act has been in effect for 13 years, the annual number of physician-assisted deaths has yet to reach 100 per year, and the annual total in Washington is even lower.

"He won the right to die without dignity."

© Mike Baldwin/Cartoonstock.com.

No Slippery Slope

The Canadian panel therefore concluded that there is strong evidence to rebut one of the greatest fears that opponents of voluntary euthanasia or physician-assisted dying often voice—that it is the first step down a slippery slope toward more widespread medical killing. The panel also found inadequate several other objections to legalization, and recommended that the law in Canada be changed to permit both physician-assisted suicide and voluntary euthanasia.

Surveys show that more than two-thirds of Canadians support legalization of voluntary euthanasia—a level that has held steady for several decades. So it is not surprising that the report received strong backing in the mainstream Canadian media. What is more puzzling is the cool response from the country's political parties, none of which indicated a willingness to support law reform in this area.

There is a similar contrast between public opinion and political (in)action elsewhere, including the United Kingdom, Australia, New Zealand, and several continental European countries. Why, when it comes to dying, do democratic institutions so often fail to translate what people want into legislation?

The Influence of Religious Institutions

I suspect that, above all, mainstream politicians fear religious institutions that oppose voluntary euthanasia, even though individual believers often do not follow their religious leaders' views. Polls in various countries have shown that a majority of Roman Catholics, for example, support legalization of voluntary euthanasia. Even in strongly Catholic Poland, more people now support legalization than oppose it.

In any case, the religious beliefs of a minority should not deny individuals like Dudley Clendinen the right to end their lives in the manner of their own choosing.

> *"Because I view life as a gift and our own lives as implicated in the lives of others, I do not believe there is a right to kill oneself."*

Liberals Should Be Wary of Assisted Suicide

E.J. Dionne

E.J. Dionne is an author, political columnist, and commentator; a political science professor at Georgetown University; and a senior fellow at the Brookings Institution. In the following viewpoint, he expresses his opposition to the right to die movement, arguing that people do not have any more right to kill themselves than they do to kill another person. Dionne contends that physician-assisted suicide is dangerous because it muddles the role and moral obligations of physicians, whose directive should always be to heal and protect, not to kill. Moreover, he is concerned that undue pressure might be placed on terminally ill and disabled people before they are ready to end their lives. Dionne does support palliative care, which could hasten the death of terminally ill patients; however, the intention of palliative care is to control pain and provide comfort to the patient, not to kill them.

As you read, consider the following questions:

1. According to Dionne, what has the death with dignity movement accomplished to help terminally ill patients?

2. What does Dionne identify as one of the maddening aspects of the fight over the Affordable Care Act?

3. What US politician fought for universal health care coverage and was then diagnosed with cancer?

You can tell how divisive an issue is when even what you name it causes controversy. In my native state of Massachusetts, Question 2 on next week's [November 2012's] ballot is called the "Death with Dignity Act" by those who support it. Those who oppose it refer to it as a measure to legalize "physician-assisted suicide." They sound very different, don't they?

The Debate

Many liberals and progressives with whom I agree on many questions support the death with dignity idea. They make two broad arguments. The first is an argument about liberty and autonomy: that the right to end one's life at a time of one's choosing is one of the most basic rights there is. Why should the government prohibit this? Why should it prevent terminally ill patients in great pain from seeking the assistance of their doctors when they know their life is nearing an end anyway? This leads to the second argument, from compassion. Why should a suffering, terminally ill person be denied the right to end his or her own suffering? And why, given the costs of our health care system, should a terminally ill person be denied the right to end his or her life and thereby save both the medical system and family members from enormous, unnecessary medical costs?

I should begin by acknowledging that my opposition to physician-assisted suicide goes "all the way down," as the philosophers like to say. Because I view life as a gift and our own lives as implicated in the lives of others, I do not believe there is a right to kill oneself. This could be described (and, by some, dismissed) as a religious view, although I believe it is defensible on nonreligious grounds. Put another way, I don't think we have any more right to kill ourselves than we do to kill other people.

I also know that most people probably disagree with me on this and might legitimately object to imposing this view of suicide through the force of law. And, in any event, my strongest objections to physician-assisted suicide do not rest on my philosophical inclinations, but on worries that many others, including liberals, might share: (1) the danger of muddling the role and the moral obligations of the doctor; (2) concern that pressure could be placed on terminally ill and disabled patients to kill themselves; and (3) a worry about how physician-assisted suicide would interact with the need to curb costs in our medical system.

Death with Dignity Accomplishments

The death with dignity movement has done enormous good by calling attention to problems in our medical system. It often did a poor job of pain management and so emphasized medical concerns, in the narrowest sense, that it dehumanized the final months of life for many terminally ill patients. Because of pressure from the death with dignity movement, there have been marked improvements on both fronts. And we need to continue moving forward.

On the issue of pain, I believe in the need to continue drawing a bright line between *risking* a patient's death by prescribing heavy doses of pain medication, and killing a patient outright. Some might dismiss this distinction as forced, but it isn't. In particular, making this distinction helps us avoid compromising the doctor's role as a healer.

Terri Schiavo

Theresa "Terri" Schiavo polarized both a nation and family with the battle over her life and death. After a 1990 heart attack left her brain damaged and in a persistent vegetative state, her husband and family eventually went to war over the possibility of her recovery. Events escalated in 2005 with an unprecedented move by the U.S. government that granted her case federal court jurisdiction. The action failed, however, as federal courts backed those of the state, and the feeding tube that had kept Schiavo alive was not reinserted. She died on March 31, 2005.

"Terri Schiavo," Gale Biography in Context, 2005.

There have also been great advances in hospice care, and we need to build on them. One of the maddening aspects of the fight over the Affordable Care Act [referring to the Patient Protection and Affordable Care Act, or Obamacare] was the explosive and false claim that the bill included "death panels." Of course it didn't. But the original bill did contain measures to encourage terminally ill patients to discuss treatment options with doctors, and to make carefully thought-through decisions as to whether they wanted to continue with heroic measures to stay alive, or to seek hospice care or other alternatives. It is a shame this part of the bill was removed and that the discussion was cut off by demagoguery. We need much more honest discussion about end-of-life care and the choices faced by those near the end of life.

Another Distinction

We need to draw another bright line between removing artificial life support and death by physician-assisted suicide. Here is where some conservatives who probably agree with my arguments went wrong on the Terri Schiavo case [a legal struggle involving keeping a woman in a vegetative state on prolonged life support]. In the case of removing support, we are acknowledging that medical advances have allowed us to trump nature and to keep someone alive long after they would otherwise have died. There is no moral obligation to keep a terminally ill patient alive through artificial, and particularly through heroic, means. In the second case, we are taking active measures to kill. I am very uneasy about erasing this line, and it is why I hope Massachusetts voters will reject Question 2.

If I would urge liberals to have second thoughts about physician-assisted suicide, I would ask conservatives who agree with me on this issue to ponder what a commitment to life means in relation to the health care system as a whole. Those lacking health insurance coverage too often cannot seek medical help until it is too late. Surely the proper moral unease they feel about physician-assisted suicide should extend to a concern for providing regular access to health care for all Americans. Emergency rooms are not the answer.

The Case of Ted Kennedy

No one fought harder for universal coverage than the late Sen. Edward M. ["Ted"] Kennedy, so I close by noting that one opponent of Question 2 is Victoria Reggie Kennedy, the senator's widow and a strong public voice in her own right. "When my husband was first diagnosed with cancer, he was told he had only two to four months to live, that he'd never get back to the United States Senate, that he should get his affairs in order, kiss his wife, love his family and get ready to die," she wrote in the *Cape Cod Times*. "But that prognosis was wrong. Teddy lived 15 more productive months."

She added: "When the end finally did come—natural death with dignity—my husband was home, attended by his doctor, surrounded by family and our priest."

Vicky Kennedy argues that the alternative to physician-assisted suicide is to "expand palliative care, pain management, nursing care and hospice." I think that is the right choice.

Periodical and Internet Sources Bibliography

The following articles have been selected to supplement the diverse views presented in this chapter.

Jerry Agar	"Euthanasia Debate Needs Thought, not Emotions," *Toronto Sun*, April 7, 2014.
Lindsey Bever	"A Tragic End for a Tiny Child Prompts Family to Campaign for Euthanasia," *Washington Post*, March 28, 2014.
Jacky Davis	"Electing When We Die Is the Ultimate Choice: It Must Be Ours and Ours Alone," *Guardian*, March 10, 2014.
Bahar Gholipour	"Should Physician-Assisted Suicide Be Legal? Poll Shows Divide Among Experts," *Huffington Post*, September 12, 2013.
Belinda Goldsmith	"British Cosmologist Hawking Backs Right to Assisted Suicide," Reuters, September 17, 2013.
Michael Gryboski	"Euthanasia, Physician-Assisted Suicide to Mirror Abortion Conflict, Says FRC Researcher," *Christian Post*, April 23, 2014.
Susan Haigh	"Assisted Suicide on Legal Agenda in Several States," Associated Press, February 8, 2013.
Jeffrey Simpson	"Assisted Suicide—The Issue We Can't Ignore," *Globe and Mail*, April 19, 2014.
Roy Speckhardt	"Getting the Freedom to Die," *Huffington Post*, April 16, 2013.
Carissa Zukowski	"Physician Assisted Suicide Should Be Legalized," *Johns Hopkins News-Letter*, April 22, 2014.

OPPOSING
VIEWPOINTS®
SERIES

CHAPTER 2

What Effect Does Euthanasia Have on Individuals and Society?

Chapter Preface

One of the most frequently cited arguments made by euthanasia opponents is that legalizing voluntary euthanasia and physician-assisted death (PAD) will lead to a slippery slope, a common logical fallacy that maintains that an idea or course of action should be stopped because there will be unwelcome consequences. In the case of euthanasia, opponents of legalization predict that if voluntary euthanasia or PAD is allowed for the terminally ill, it will eventually be legal and socially acceptable for other patients, including those with treatable conditions, physical or mental disabilities, or severe depression.

Proponents of the slippery slope argument point to examples of controversial cases in recent years to back up their claims. One of the most publicized was the case of Marc and Eddy Verbessem, forty-five-year-old twin brothers from Putte, Belgium. Deaf from birth, the brothers had created their own special sign language and could not communicate with the outside world. They had lived together their entire adult lives, working as cobblers and taking care of one another. However, when doctors informed them that glaucoma and other severe health problems would eventually cause them both to go blind, Marc and Eddy decided that they did not want to live any longer.

In Belgium, there are three qualifications for approval to be euthanized: an applicant must be suffering from a hopeless medical condition; have a serious and incurable accidental or pathological condition; or endure constant and unbearable physical or mental pain that cannot be relieved. To be approved, a family physician must determine that the patient is eligible for the procedure. Then, an independent physician must be consulted to make sure the candidate fits the criteria and that the patient has a sound and informed mind. Unless the patient is near death, a third physician—a psychiatrist or specialist in the patient's condition—is then called in to give an evaluation.

The case of the Verbessem brothers was unusual. In Belgium, most of the applicants for euthanasia approval suffer from terminal illness or are in unbearable physical pain. Marc and Eddy, however, were not. Their disease would cause them to go blind, but it would not cause severe pain or result in death. For them, the pain would be psychological. Without the ability to communicate with one another, and to be further isolated from the outside world, would be unbearable.

Initially, their application for assisted suicide was rejected by their local hospital. Doctors there did not find that they would be suffering from intolerable pain. After a couple of years, however, Marc and Eddy found doctors at another hospital to approve their application. On December 14, 2012, the Verbessem brothers were lethally injected, together and surrounded by family.

The case of the Verbessem brothers is often cited by opponents of euthanasia as an example of the slippery slope of the legalization of assisted death. Marc and Eddy were not terminally ill nor in unbearable physical torment. To interpret their particular situation as intolerable and worthy of death is misguided and dangerous, these critics argue. Some suggest that the brothers could have learned to live with their disability and found meaning in their lives despite their hardships.

Others counter that by allowing the brothers to die through assisted means, they were permitted one last act of self-determination and the right to die with dignity. If they were committed to ending their lives, it was better to be in a controlled, humane setting under medical supervision and surrounded by family than to die alone through suicide.

The controversial case of the Verbessem brothers and the argument of the slippery slope is one of the topics explored in the following chapter, which considers the effects of euthanasia on individuals and society. Other viewpoints in the chapter discuss the morality of euthanasia, its relationship to the value of human life, and how civilized societies should treat such sensitive issues as life, death, and the process of dying.

> "This seems to me quite a reasonable and sensible decision for someone with a serious, incurable and debilitating disease to elect for a medically assisted death by appointment."

Euthanasia Is Merciful and Reasonable

Terry Pratchett

Terry Pratchett is a prolific and popular author and activist. In the following viewpoint, he outlines his position in the contentious debate over euthanasia and physician-assisted death in Great Britain that he became involved in after his diagnosis with posterior cortical atrophy (PCA), a form of Alzheimer's disease. Pratchett favors the term "assisted death" because he believes that for most people, the decision to end one's life by medical means is usually the result of careful deliberation. As such, society should respect a patient's well-considered decision to pursue assisted death. He proposes that the government consider a euthanasia tribunal, which would be responsible for protecting vulnerable patients, but would be reasonable enough not to stand in the way of those who have come to a well-informed decision about the end of their lives. He suggests himself as a test case for the tribunal, expressing his wish to die peacefully, in his own home, with the help of a doctor.

As you read, consider the following questions:

1. How does the author say that posterior cortical atrophy (PCA) manifests itself?

2. According to a 2007 article in the *Journal of Medical Ethics*, was there any evidence that vulnerable patients were being forced to submit to assisted suicide in Oregon?

3. How old does Pratchett think that members of the euthanasia tribunal must be to be wise and compassionate enough to make such major end-of-life decisions?

When I was a young boy, playing on the floor of my grandmother's front room, I glanced up at the television and saw Death, talking to a knight. I didn't know much about death at that point. It was the thing that happened to budgerigars and hamsters. But it was Death, with a scythe and an amiable manner. I didn't know it at the time, of course, but I had just watched a clip from Ingmar Bergman's *The Seventh Seal*, wherein the knight engages in protracted dialogue, and of course the famous chess game, with the Grim Reaper who, it seemed to me, did not seem so terribly grim.

The image has remained with me ever since and Death as a character appeared in the first of my Discworld novels. He has evolved in the series to be one of its most popular characters; implacable, because that is his job, he appears to have some sneaking regard and compassion for a race of creatures which are to him as ephemeral as mayflies, but which nevertheless spend their brief lives making rules for the universe and counting the stars.

Family Memories

I have no clear recollection of the death of my grandparents, but my paternal grandfather died in the ambulance on the way to hospital after just having cooked and eaten his own dinner at the age of 96. He had felt very odd, got a neighbour to ring for the doctor and stepped tidily into the ambulance and out of the world. A good death if ever there was one. Except that, according to my father, he did complain to the ambulance men that he hadn't had time to finish his pudding. I am not at all sure about the truth of this, because my father had a finely tuned sense of humour that he was good enough to bequeath to me, presumably to make up for the weak bladder, short stature and male pattern baldness which regrettably came with the package.

My father's own death was more protracted. He had a year's warning. It was pancreatic cancer. Technology kept him alive, at home and in a state of reasonable comfort and cheerfulness, for that year, during which we had those conversations that you have with a dying parent. Perhaps it is when you truly get to know them, when you realise that it is now you marching towards the sound of the guns and you are ready to listen to the advice and reminiscences that life was too crowded for up to that point. He unloaded all the anecdotes that I had heard before, about his time in India during the war, and came up with a few more that I had never heard. Then, at one point, he suddenly looked up and said, "I can feel the sun of India on my face", and his face did light up rather magically, brighter and happier than I had seen it at any time in the previous year, and if there had been any justice or even narrative sensibility in the universe, he would have died there and then, shading his eyes from the sun of Karachi.

He did not.

On the day he was diagnosed my father told me, "If you ever see me in a hospital bed, full of tubes and pipes and no good to anybody, tell them to switch me off." In fact, it took something under a fortnight in the hospice for him to die as a kind of collateral damage in the war between his cancer and the morphine. And in that time he stopped being him and started becoming a corpse, albeit one that moved ever so slightly from time to time.

The Arrival of Alzheimer's Disease

On the way back home after my father's death I scraped my Jag along a stone wall in Hay-on-Wye. To be fair, it's almost impossible not to scrape Jags along the walls in Hay-on-Wye even if your eyes aren't clouded with tears, but what I didn't know at the time, but strongly suspect now, was that also playing a part in that little accident was my own disease, subtly making its presence felt.

When the specialist gave me the news that I had posterior cortical atrophy [PCA], a rare form of Alzheimer's disease, I quite genuinely saw him outlined in a rectangle of flaming red lines. The whole world had changed.

PCA manifests itself through sight problems, and difficulty with topological tasks, such as buttoning up a shirt. I have the opposite of a superpower; sometimes I cannot see what is there. I see the teacup with my eyes, but my brain refuses to send me the teacup message. It's very Zen. First, there is no teacup and then, because I know there is a teacup, the teacup will appear the next time I look. I have little work-arounds to deal with this sort of thing—people with PCA live in a world of work-arounds.

If you did not know there was anything wrong with me, you would not know there is anything wrong with me. The disease moves slowly, but you know it's there. Imagine a very, very slow-motion car crash. Nothing much seems to be happening. There's an occasional little bang, a crunch, a screw pops out and spins across the dashboard as if we're in Apollo 13. But the radio is still playing, the heater is on and it doesn't seem all that bad, except for the certain knowledge that sooner or later you will definitely be going headfirst through the windscreen.

Assisted Death

I have heard it said that some people feel they are being avoided once the news gets around that they have Alzheimer's. For me it has been just the reverse. People want to talk to me—on city streets, in theatre queues, on aeroplanes over the Atlantic, even on country walks. They want to tell me about their mother, their husband, their grandmother. Increasingly, they want to talk about what I prefer to call "assisted death", but which is still called, wrongly in my opinion, "assisted suicide".

As a pallid and nervous young journalist, I got to know about suicide. It was part of my regular tasks to sit in at the coroner's court, where I learned all the manifold ways the disturbed human brain can devise to die. Newspapers were a little more kindly in those days, and we tended not to go into too much detail, but I had to listen to it. And I remember that coroners never used the word "insanity". They preferred the more compassionate verdict that the subject had "taken his life while the balance of his mind was disturbed". There was ambivalence to the phrase, a suggestion of the winds of fate and overwhelming circumstance.

In fact, by now, I have reached the conclusion that a person may make a decision to die because the balance of their mind is level, realistic, pragmatic, stoic and sharp. And that is why I dislike the term "assisted suicide" applied to the carefully thought-out and weighed-up process of having one's life ended by gentle medical means.

The people who thus far have made the harrowing trip to Dignitas in Switzerland to die seemed to me to be very firm and methodical of purpose, with a clear prima facie case for wanting their death to be on their own terms. In short, their minds may well be in better balance than the world around them.

And once again I remember my father. He did not want to die a curious kind of living death. He wasn't that kind of person. He wanted to say goodbye to me, and knowing him, he would probably have finished with a joke of some sort. And if the nurses had put the relevant syringe in the cannula, I would have pressed it, and felt it was my duty. There would have been tears, of course there would; tears would be appropriate and insuppressible.

The Debate

I got involved in the debate surrounding "assisted death" by accident after taking a long and informed look at my future as someone with Alzheimer's and subsequently writing an article about my conclusions. As a result of my "coming out" about the disease, I now have contacts in medical research industries all over the world, and I have no reason to believe that a "cure" is imminent. I do think, on their good advice, that there may be some very interesting developments in the next couple of years and I'm not the only one to hope for some kind of stepping stone—a treatment that will keep me going long enough for a better treatment to be developed.

Back in my early reporting days, I was told that nobody has to do what the doctor tells them. I learned this when chief reporter George Topley slung my copy back at me and said, "Never say that a patient has been released from hospital unless you are talking about someone who is being detained on mental grounds. The proper word is 'discharged', and even though the staff would like you to believe that you just can't walk out until they say so, you damn well can. Although, generally speaking, it's best not to be dragging a portable life support system down the steps with you." George was a remarkable journalist who as a fiery young man would have fought

The Career of Terry Pratchett

Called the "master of humorous fantasy" by a critic for *Publishers Weekly*, British author Terry Pratchett won the prestigious Carnegie Medal in 2002 for his novel *The Amazing Maurice and His Educated Rodents*. Author of numerous science fiction and fantasy novels, Pratchett is known primarily for his Discworld series—over two dozen strong and growing—and his Bromeliad trilogy for children. Critic David V. Barrett stated ... that the novels of Discworld "are works of marvelous composition and rattling good stories." "Pratchett is an acquired taste," wrote a critic for *Publishers Weekly* in a review of the Discworld novel *Interesting Times*, "but the acquisition seems easy, judging from the robust popularity of Discworld." Discworld—as well as most of Pratchett's other works—also offers humorous parodies of other famous science fiction and fantasy writers ... and spoofs such modern trends as New Age philosophy and universal concerns like death. Nevertheless, "in among the slapstick and clever word-play are serious concepts," as Barrett pointed out. In "genres assailed by shoddiness, mediocrity, and ... the endless series," asserted *Locus* critic Faren Miller in a review of *Witches Abroad*, "Pratchett is never shoddy, and under the laughter there's a far from mediocre mind at work."

"Terry Pratchett,"
Gale Biography in Context, 2009.

fascism in the Spanish Civil War were it not for the fact that he stowed away on the wrong boat and ended up in Hull.

I remember what George said and vowed that rather than let Alzheimer's take me, I would take it. I would live my life as ever to the full and die, before the disease mounted its last attack, in my own home, in a chair on the lawn, with a brandy in my hand to wash down whatever modern version of the "Brompton cocktail" [an elixir meant for use as a pain suppressant] some helpful medic could supply. And with Thomas Tallis on my iPod, I would shake hands with Death.

This seems to me quite a reasonable and sensible decision for someone with a serious, incurable and debilitating disease to elect for a medically assisted death by appointment. These days, nontraumatic death—deaths that don't, for example, involve several cars, a tanker and a patch of ice on the M4 [a road in England]—largely take place in hospitals and hospices. Not so long ago, they took place in your own bed. The Victorians knew how to die. They saw a lot of death. And Victorian and Edwardian London were awash with what we would call recreational drugs, which were seen as a boon and a blessing to all. Departing on schedule with the help of a friendly doctor was quite usual.

Does that still apply? It would seem so. Did the Victorians fear death? As Death says in one of my own books, most men don't fear death, they fear those things—the knife, the shipwreck, the illness, the bomb—that proceed, by microseconds if you're lucky and many years if you're not, the moment of death.

Care or Killing

And this brings us into the whole care or killing argument.

The Care Not Killing alliance assures us that no one need consider a voluntary death of any sort since care is always available. This is questionable. Medicine is keeping more and more people alive, all requiring more and more care. Alzheimer's and other dementias place a huge care burden on the country, a burden that falls initially on the next of kin, who may even be elderly and, indeed, be in need of some sort of care themselves.

A major objection frequently flourished by opponents of assisted dying is that elderly people might be illegally persuaded into "asking" for assisted death. Could be, but the *Journal of Medical Ethics* reported in 2007 that there was no evidence of the abuse of vulnerable patients in Oregon, where assisted dying is currently legal. I don't see why things should be any different here.

Last year [2009], the government finally published guidelines on dealing with assisted death. They did not appear to satisfy anybody. It seems that those wishing to assist a friend or relative to die would have to meet quite a large number of criteria in order to escape the chance of prosecution for murder. We should be thankful that there is, in theory, some possibility that they might not be prosecuted but, as laid out, the best anyone can do is keep within the rules and hope for the best.

The Proposal

That is why I and others have suggested some kind of strictly nonaggressive tribunal that would establish the facts of the case well before the assisted death takes place. This might make some people, including me, a little uneasy as it suggests the government has the power to tell you whether you can live or die. But, that said, the government cannot sidestep the responsibility to ensure the protection of the vulnerable and we must respect that. It grieves me that those against assisted death seem to assume, as a matter of course, that those of us who support it have not thought long and hard about this very issue. It is, in fact, at the soul and centre of my argument.

The members of the tribunal would be acting for the good of society as well as that of the applicant—horrible word—to ensure they are of sound and informed mind, firm in their purpose, suffering from a life-threatening and incurable disease and not under the influence of a third party. It would need wiser heads than mine, though heaven knows they should be easy enough to find, to determine how such tribunals are constituted. But I would suggest there should be a lawyer, one with expertise in dynastic family affairs who has become good at recognising what somebody really means, and indeed if there is outside pressure. And a medical practitioner experienced in dealing with the complexities of serious long-term illnesses.

I would also suggest that all those on the tribunal are over 45, by which time they may have acquired the rare gift of wisdom, because wisdom and compassion should, in this tribunal, stand side by side with the law. The tribunal would also have to be a check on those seeking death for reasons that reasonable people may consider trivial or transient distress. I dare say that quite a few people have contemplated death for reasons that much later seemed to them to be quite minor. If we are to live in a world where a socially acceptable "early death" can be allowed, it must be allowed as a result of careful consideration.

Let us consider me as a test case. As I have said, I would like to die peacefully with Thomas Tallis on my iPod before the disease takes me over and I hope that will not be for quite some time to come, because if I knew that I could die at any time I wanted, then suddenly every day would be as precious as a million pounds. If I knew that I could die, I would live. My life, my death, my choice.

> "How foolish to believe that we can or even should dictate to death or, worse, that dying amidst excruciating pain, as our faculties disappear, as we become more helpless than babies, is somehow an undignified end."

Euthanasia Is Barbarous and Immoral

Rosie DiManno

Rosie DiManno is a columnist for the Toronto Star. *In the following viewpoint, she expresses her extreme disappointment that there is a serious movement to legalize euthanasia and physician-assisted death in Canada and other Western countries. DiManno argues that allowing euthanasia is immoral because it devalues life, and she says that because the process of dying is part of living, it has intrinsic value as part of life's journey. In her opinion, no one should be able to choose the moment of their death. She is concerned about any society that treats the disabled, elderly, and terminally ill as expendable, unaffordable, or inconvenient. She also is concerned that legalizing euthanasia for terminally ill patients will eventually lead to a slippery slope. As evidence, she points to countries that have considered legalizing euthanasia for terminally ill children and the disabled.*

As you read, consider the following questions:

1. According to the author, what Canadian province struck down the criminal code provision against euthanasia?

2. What generation does DiManno blame for catapulting the debate about euthanasia to the forefront of Western consciousness?

3. What country was the second in the world to legalize euthanasia for adults, according to the author?

I went to my Uncle Valentino's funeral the other day. He died just a couple weeks short of his 88th birthday, leaving a wife to whom he'd been married for 67 years, two daughters, grandchildren, great-grandchildren and the legacy of a generous life well lived.

After several months of painful struggle and with amputation of both feet looming—which he'd steadfastly refused—Valentino fell finally into a deep, peaceful sleep and didn't wake up. His family had never left his side, not only because the gravely ill need the constant presence of an advocate when hospitalized but also because they did not want to miss a single treasured hour of a life draining away.

Despite the suffering, not once to my knowledge did Uncle Val ever express a wish to depart this earth, to hurry up his leave-taking because the pain of living had become too great.

I like to think that Valentino willed himself to die, in the end. He was done. And this is the only form of self-extinction I can morally abide.

My own father, through half a year of hospitalization and multiple surgeries, was in unbearable agony in his final weeks of consciousness. He screamed from the pain and I screamed watching it. But when he begged to make it stop, he didn't mean "end my life." And it never crossed my mind to think, "Kill off this man as an act of kindness."

What I wanted to do was kill the medical men and women around him who were failing so monstrously to alleviate his pain. My father did not need assisted suicide. He needed assistance to manage end-of-life traumas that assaulted his body.

An Immoral Debate

We are all so desperately afraid of pain and burdening those we love. We are increasingly adopting the euphemistic vocabulary of assisted suicide as if phrases like "dying with dignity" mean anything in the real world, drawing outrageous comparisons to animals put down as a mercy that should be extended to human beings. In fact, we destroy our aged and ill pets to extinguish our own distress, the messiness of tending to a needy creature.

I do not kill my animals. I've lain down with them, held them, waited for dogs and cats to draw their last breath.

We are not animals, though that might be a moral improvement.

An Immutable Truth

It is repugnant that we are now discussing doing away with the elderly, the diseased, the terminally ill, those whose "quality of life"—a dreadful expression—has been deemed unendurable.

We forget what every other generation before this one has understood in its bones: That dying, with all its miseries, is a part of living; that we do not and should not get to choose the moment of our death any more than we chose the moment of our birth; and that those who exist in the shadowy realm between life and death are in a state of grace, which is the gift they give us—to witness and *feel* this existential dimension, this passage. It is a spiritualism few of us would otherwise experience and it matters not if you're a person of faith or an atheist.

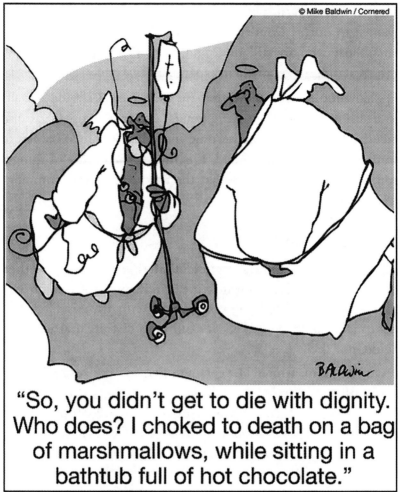

"So, you didn't get to die with dignity. Who does? I choked to death on a bag of marshmallows, while sitting in a bathtub full of hot chocolate."

© Mike Baldwin/Cartoonstock.com.

I am dismayed about where this assisted-suicide public debate will lead us as a society, with Quebec already tabling legislation that would allow physicians to hasten death and British Columbia earlier striking down the criminal code provision against euthanasia, a decision now under appeal.

The public's apparent eagerness to embrace the ethically profane is being driven by a generation of baby boomers who, throughout their lives, have become accustomed to setting the moral template by which everybody else must abide. Now, as they slouch toward twilight, the dying of the light, they don't want it to hurt. I wonder about their frail and dependent parents, those who are still alive, and what they must think about the escalating tenor of their expendability.

How foolish to believe that we can or even should dictate to death or, worse, that dying amidst excruciating pain, as our faculties disappear, as we become more helpless than babies, is somehow an undignified end. It is merely the nature of things, sometimes, and it's nature that the assisted-suicide promoters wish to defy.

A Slippery Slope

Do not for one minute pretend that this is anything other than a slippery slope towards the annihilation of human beings who tax our willingness to cope with the disabled, the deformed, the grievously ill. It's our own distress that we can't abide, not theirs.

In Belgium, which 11 years ago became the second country in the world to legalize euthanasia for adults, 2 per cent of deaths annually occur in this manner. Now Belgian politicians are debating an amendment to the law that would make it the first country to legalize euthanasia of children of any age in cases of "unbearable and irreversible" suffering. Unbearable to whom? Palliative sedation is available for these youngsters but some parents want a quicker and "merciful" end. These are not youngsters who can express their own wishes.

In the Netherlands, children between the ages of 12 and 16 can already request euthanasia, with a parent's permission.

The parameters are less restrictive than you might think. Last year [2012], twin Belgian brothers in their early 40s requested euthanasia because they were both deaf and going slowly blind. It was granted. Euthanasia has also been granted to patients with chronic depression or with the early signs of Alzheimer's [disease].

In Canada we have doctors with a god complex fighting for the legal right to decide when life-sustaining treatment should be withdrawn, even over the objections of a patient's family.

But these are not just decisions that individuals make for themselves or on behalf of dependents and loved ones incapable of formulating the answer: No. Every erosion of the principle that all life is sacred, no matter the infirmities or "indignities," adds to the manifest disregard, the impatience, with those whose limited existence is deemed less worthy, intolerable and an encumbrance. It dilutes the time-immemorial taboos against taking a life.

This is not mercy. It is barbarous.

"*[Euthanasia in the Netherlands] is an onerous task for the attending physician, and it also demands paperwork and careful planning. Demands for euthanasia are not made lightly and are more often denied than granted, largely because of insufficient forethought.*"

Euthanasia Respects Individual Autonomy and Requires Deliberation

Mars Cramer

Mars Cramer is a writer, political and social commentator, and former econometrics professor. In the following viewpoint, he recounts his wife's struggle with a rare cancer, her decision to end her life, and the careful process of euthanasia in the Netherlands. Cramer chronicles the legal steps that his wife, Mathilde, had to fulfill before she was allowed to pursue the option: authorities had to be satisfied that she earnestly desired euthanasia; she had to find a respected doctor who would perform the procedure; it had to be determined that she was suffering from a terminal illness and was in unbearable pain; and she had to prove that she was of sound and informed mind. Cramer emphasizes how important it was for his wife to maintain her autonomy until the very end, even taking great pains to arrange the details of her final moments of life. He concludes that euthanasia was the right decision for both her and her family.

As you read, consider the following questions:

1. What does the author list as the chief danger of Waldenström's disease?

2. According to a recent study, what percentage of Dutch family doctors have performed euthanasia at least once?

3. According to the viewpoint, how often were problematic requests for euthanasia referred to a special monitoring committee for further assessment in 2010?

I was living in comfortable retirement with my wife, Mathilde, when, at the age of 71, she received a diagnosis of Waldenström's disease. The chief danger of this rare cancer of the bone marrow is that it impedes and eventually destroys the production of vital components of the blood supply.

It was held at bay by periodic bouts of chemotherapy, sometimes for a few months, once for several years. And for a long time, we lived our lives under this regime, citizens of the realm of the chronically ill, with monthly visits to the cancer hospital for checks and tests, always wary of the disease. But this soon became a routine, and for long spells we did not feel seriously threatened, taking a quick holiday when another round of chemotherapy was in the offing. Apart from fatigue and the common effects of advancing age, Mathilde did not suffer very much.

A Turning Point

Then, after seven years, the cancer suddenly turned aggressive and the treatment no longer worked. The disease had soon wrought havoc among the leukocytes, the white blood cells that guard against infection, and all of Mathilde's resistance had gone. It was just a matter of time—a couple of weeks or maybe months—before she would die from influenza or some other common infection. At the hospital, they gave her a blood transfusion and told her to report next week; and then they gave her another blood transfusion and told her to report again a week later. And if she had not fallen ill and refused further treatment, they would no doubt have continued in this way.

But we live in the Netherlands, and here is where our story becomes a little different. When people become as ill as my wife, with no prospect of cure and only pain and exhaustion in the offing, it is quite legal to end one's life by voluntary euthanasia.

For all her quiet ways, Mathilde was a strong-willed person, cherishing her independence and her freedom, and determined to live her life as she wanted. When euthanasia first became a public issue in the early 1970s, she became a strong supporter of the cause. We joined the Dutch Association for Voluntary Euthanasia, signed petitions and wrote letters to members of Parliament demanding such a law. When, as a first step, our courts set out conditions that made euthanasia acceptable, Mathilde, then only in her 40s, made sure we filled out the forms with the association stating that we wanted to receive euthanasia when the time came.

In 2001, euthanasia finally was fully legalized. Those who wanted it had to ensure the cooperation of their family doctor. We made sure all the doctors who joined our village medical practice knew our wishes, and we always asked whether they would administer euthanasia. As an added precaution, Mathilde continued to carry a thick wad of forms and declarations in her handbag wherever she went, in case of an accident.

All the doctors agreed to our request. They were from a younger generation; it is older doctors, mainly, who are reluc-

Euthanasia in the Netherlands

In 1981, courts in the Netherlands ruled that euthanasia was "acceptable," meaning that though it was illegal, a doctor who helped end a suffering patient's life would not be prosecuted if he or she had followed specific guidelines. Under these guidelines, euthanasia and physician-assisted suicide were practiced on a regular basis in the Netherlands for two decades. In April 2001, the Netherlands became the first nation to legalize euthanasia and physician-assisted suicide. By 2008, active euthanasia was legal in the Netherlands, Belgium, and Luxembourg. Assisted suicide was legal in Switzerland and in the states of Oregon and Washington in the United States.

"Assisted Suicide and Euthanasia,"
Global Issues in Context Online Collection, 2014.

tant to administer euthanasia. A few refuse on grounds of principle, others because they just do not wish to become involved. But more than 80 percent of all Dutch family doctors, according to a recent large study, report that they have performed euthanasia at least once, and among the willing doctors the average rate is once every two or three years.

Euthanasia is by now widely accepted here. It is supported by the vast majority of the population, of the medical profession and of the political parties. The costs for it are borne by our compulsory health insurance, and suicide clauses voiding life insurance policies have been set aside. Still, it is an onerous task for the attending physician, and it also demands paperwork and careful planning. Demands for euthanasia are not made lightly and are more often denied than granted, largely because of insufficient forethought.

But in Mathilde's case, forethought had not been lacking.

Waiting to Fall Ill

When it was clear that Mathilde's life was coming to its end, we went at once to see our doctor and reminded him of his earlier promise to administer euthanasia. I asked him how it was done. In the past, he told us, the patient drank a deadly potion, demonstrating for the last time the exercise of free will. But that is an uncertain method: Sometimes the patient throws up and survives in worse shape than before. More certain is the active method, where the doctor prepares two syringes. The first injection induces a deep coma; the second is a muscle relaxant that stops the heart. The whole process is over in a couple of minutes.

We still had a couple of weeks, perhaps a month or two, before things came to that. We informed our children, all adult now, our relatives and close friends, and then we settled down to wait.

There were three possible places for Mathilde's death: the hospital, a local hospice and at home, in her own bed. She chose the last option and began her preparations, taking off her wedding ring of more than 50 years and issuing firm instructions: I should be present when she died; if euthanasia were used, I must be at her bedside and our children nearby, in the house but not in the bedroom.

And contrary to what is common here, she wanted her body to be taken away before nightfall, not lying in state for several days for friends and relatives to pay their last respects, a custom Mathilde and I both disliked.

In all these matters I accepted her wishes without argument, as I was wont to do, for I knew how much she disliked tiresome explanations and discussions.

All her life, Mathilde had slept soundly, falling asleep like a contented child, and until her very last days she continued to do so. I slept at her side, not so soundly, with instructions about what to do should she die in her sleep (a vain hope):

Close her eyes, prop up her chin ("Otherwise, my mouth will fall open and I shall look silly") and only then call the doctor.

Every morning, Mathilde would take her temperature. One day she ran a fever, and soon she became very ill indeed. First she contracted influenza but miraculously recovered; then there followed cystitis. She kept to her bed, and when another blood transfusion was due, she refused to go. She had given up. She no longer slept well and no longer wanted food or drink. The time had come to act.

Euthanasia Guidelines

The law lists four major conditions for euthanasia. It must be administered by a doctor; the patient must earnestly desire it, a resolve taken after due deliberation, and freely; there must be no prospect of recovery and, in the words of the law, the patient must be suffering unbearably. The attending physician must confirm that these conditions are met and write a report to this effect.

As a rule, the family doctor who has known the patient for years is the best judge of her condition and of the earnestness and independence of her request. But he must also consult another doctor, an outsider, for an independent assessment; that doctor must also put his views in writing. Afterward, both reports are submitted to a monitoring committee, which may ask for further explanation and can refer problematic cases to the inspector of health and the public prosecutor. But their annual reports show that the monitoring committees do this only very rarely—in 2010, at the rate of one in every 300 reported cases.

We called for the consulting doctor, who spent the better part of an hour with Mathilde. Afterward, he called our family doctor and said he was not sure she was suffering enough.

What is unbearable suffering? It is an impossible question. The monitoring committees have given up trying to define it and adopted the view that the patient's own judgment is decisive, provided the acting doctor is convinced of its earnestness and sincerity. For Mathilde, the prospect of being at the mercy of random infections while permanently dependent on blood transfusions was intolerable. We wrote a letter to this effect and heard no more of it.

Mathilde's Death

On a Sunday morning not long afterward, we decided that the time had come. The logistics dictated a tight schedule. The doctor had to order the drugs, which meant a day's delay. On Tuesday, he would be available at the earliest in the afternoon, after his morning rounds. Afterward, we would have to wait for a visit from the coroner, since Mathilde would have died an unnatural death, and only after that could the undertaker take the body away.

We set the date for Tuesday at 3 p.m. Our children assembled in the sitting room and I was in the bedroom, with the doctor and a nurse. Mathilde had had a bad night, distraught and unable to sleep, and the doctor had come to give her morphine.

But now she was awake and fully conscious of her condition. To the nurse she said, "I am ready" and to me, "I am not afraid." I sat on one side of the bed and took her hand, and the doctor, at the other side, gave her the first injection.

She immediately fell asleep, snoring loudly. The doctor gave her a second injection, and the snoring stopped. She had died. It was all over in a couple of minutes.

What about emotions? Was there no grief, no anguish, was it all a matter of procedures and logistics?

Oh, yes, I felt plenty of grief in those terrible weeks. I had loved my wife more than anything else in the world, day by day, for over 50 years, and to know that she would shortly die was breaking my heart. But at the supreme moment, did our eyes meet in a last loving look? Were we united by a sense of extraordinary belonging and togetherness?

Nothing of the kind. By this time Mathilde was very ill and running a fever. Events demanded her utmost concentration, and quite understandably she had no time for me. And I, who had been crying for weeks, who had burst into tears at my appointment with the dentist when that kind man asked me in all innocence how I was, at this ultimate moment I felt nothing beyond the constant numbing grief of the last weeks.

The Aftermath

I saw the doctor out, and one of our daughters went to dress her mother as she had wanted.

Then my children left, the nurse withdrew and I sat alone in the living room. The coroner, who had been alerted by the doctor, called to say that he was held up in traffic. When he arrived, he stomped up the stairs and down again, and gave me a sheaf of legal papers. "Do not read them," he said. "Just hand them to the undertaker." I called the undertaker and told him we were ready.

And then, as I sat there by myself, all the formalities completed, I began to wonder whether I was right in not taking a last look at my wife in death. I reflected that many people derive comfort and solace from the practice, and I also recalled a passage from the memoirs of some British author who had also lost his wife in old age and in illness, like me. When he went to view her body, he reported that she had in death quite miraculously regained the radiance of her youth.

Three times I went upstairs to take a look. Mathilde was lying there peacefully, quite cold, even colder than the room, so it seemed. She looked no younger than she was when she died. Again I felt no particular emotion. The British author must have been a fool.

It was already dark when the undertaker's men arrived. It did not take them long to take Mathilde away.

The day was over, and all her wishes had been fulfilled.

> *"Most people, regardless of religious affiliation, know that suicide is a terrible tragedy, one that a compassionate society should work to prevent."*

Euthanasia Devalues Human Life and Limits Individual Freedom

United States Conference of Catholic Bishops

The United States Conference of Catholic Bishops (USCCB) is the official organization for all active and retired members of the Roman Catholic hierarchy. In the following viewpoint, the group rejects the legalization of euthanasia and physician-assisted suicide, explaining that a caring community protects its most vulnerable members and defends the sacred gift of life. To that end, palliative care is the moral and compassionate option for those struggling valiantly with terminal disease or severe disability. The movement to legalize euthanasia does not enhance freedom or self-determination because many of those fighting to kill themselves are depressed and need treatment or may be unduly influenced by familial, societal, or institutional pressures to end their lives. Furthermore, one cannot enhance human freedom and dignity by devaluing human life, the bishops explain.

As you read, consider the following questions:

1. To what has the Hemlock Society changed its name, according to the viewpoint?

2. According to the author, in what year did the US Supreme Court reject the claims that there is a constitutional right to assisted suicide?

3. What groups do Dutch doctors now provide lethal drugs to for physician-assisted death, according to the viewpoint?

To live in a manner worthy of our human dignity, and to spend our final days on this earth in peace and comfort, surrounded by loved ones—that is the hope of each of us. In particular, Christian hope sees these final days as a time to prepare for our eternal destiny.

Today, however, many people fear the dying process. They are afraid of being kept alive past life's natural limits by burdensome medical technology. They fear experiencing intolerable pain and suffering, losing control over bodily functions, or lingering with severe dementia. They worry about being abandoned or becoming a burden on others.

Our society can be judged by how we respond to these fears. A caring community devotes more attention, not less, to members facing the most vulnerable times in their lives. When people are tempted to see their own lives as diminished in value or meaning, they most need the love and assistance of others to assure them of their inherent worth.

The healing art of medicine is an important part of this assistance. Even when a cure is not possible, medicine plays a critical role in providing "palliative care"—alleviating pain and other symptoms and meeting basic needs. Such care should combine medical skill with attention to the emotional as well as spiritual needs of those facing the end of life.

A Renewed Threat to Human Dignity

Today there is a campaign to respond to these fears and needs in a radically different way. It uses terms like "death with dignity" to describe a self-inflicted death, generally using a drug overdose prescribed by a doctor for the purpose of suicide.

This campaign to legalize doctor-prescribed suicide has been rejected by most policy makers in our society. Although Oregon passed a law in 1994 allowing physicians to prescribe deadly drugs for some patients, similar proposals were rejected by legislatures and voters in all other states for many years. The claim of a constitutional right to assisted suicide was firmly rejected in 1997 by the U.S. Supreme Court, which upheld state laws against the practice as legitimate safeguards for innocent human life and the ethical integrity of medicine.

But after fourteen years of defeats, the assisted suicide campaign advanced its agenda when Washington State passed a law like Oregon's in 2008. The following year, Montana's highest court suggested that physician-assisted suicide for terminally ill patients is not always against public policy. [In 2013, Vermont passed legislation legalizing physician-assisted suicide.] With expanded funding from wealthy donors, assisted-suicide proponents have renewed their aggressive nationwide campaign through legislation, litigation, and public advertising, targeting states they see as most susceptible to their message.

If they succeed, society will undergo a radical change. Jewish and Christian moral traditions have long rejected the idea of assisting in another's suicide. Catholic teaching views suicide as a grave offense against love of self, one that also breaks the bonds of love and solidarity with family, friends, and God. To assist another's suicide is to take part in "an injustice which can never be excused, even if it is requested" (John Paul II, *Evangelium Vitae*, no. 66). Most people, regardless of religious affiliation, know that suicide is a terrible tragedy, one that a compassionate society should work to prevent. They realize that allowing doctors to prescribe the means for their patients to kill themselves is a corruption of the healing art. It even violates the Hippocratic Oath that has guided physicians for millennia: "I will not give a lethal drug to anyone if I am asked, nor will I advise such a plan."

Proponents know these facts, so they avoid terms such as "assisting suicide" and instead use euphemisms such as "aid in dying." The organization leading this campaign has even concealed its agenda by changing its name. The Hemlock Society, whose very name reminded people of the harsh reality of death by poison, has become "Compassion & Choices."

Plain speaking is needed to strip away this veneer and uncover what is at stake, for this agenda promotes neither free choice nor compassion.

The Illusion of Freedom

Does the drive to legalize physician-assisted suicide really enhance choices or freedom for people with serious health conditions? No, it does not, for several reasons.

First, medical professionals recognize that people who take their own lives commonly suffer from a mental illness, such as clinical depression. Suicidal desires may be triggered by very real setbacks and serious disappointments in life. However, suicidal persons become increasingly incapable of appreciating options for dealing with these problems, suffering from a kind of tunnel vision that sees relief only in death. They need help to be *freed from* their suicidal thoughts through counseling and support and, when necessary and helpful, medication. Because the illnesses that cause or aggravate suicidal desires are often overlooked or misdiagnosed, many civil laws provide for psychological evaluation and treatment for those who have attempted suicide. The Catholic Church, as well, recognizes that "grave psychological disturbances, anguish, or grave fear of hardship, suffering, or torture" can diminish the responsibility of people committing suicide; the church encourages Catholics to pray for them, trusting in God's mercy.

These statements about psychological disturbance and diminished responsibility are also true of people who attempt suicide during serious illness. Yet this is often ignored in proposals authorizing assistance in these individuals' suicides. Many such proposals permit—but do not require—an evaluation for mental illness or depression before lethal drugs are prescribed. In practice such evaluations are rare, and even a finding of mental illness or depression does not necessarily prevent prescribing the drugs. No evaluation is done at the time the drugs are actually taken.

In fact, such laws have generally taken great care to *avoid* real scrutiny of the process for doctor-prescribed death—or any inquiry into *whose* choice is served. In Oregon and Washington, for example, all reporting is done solely by the physician who prescribes lethal drugs. Once they are prescribed, the law requires no assessment of whether patients are acting freely, whether they are influenced by those who have financial or other motives for ensuring their death, or even whether others actually administer the drugs. Here the line between assisted suicide and homicide becomes blurred.

People who request death are vulnerable. They need care and protection. To offer them lethal drugs is a victory not for freedom but for the worst form of neglect. Such abandonment is especially irresponsible when society is increasingly aware of elder abuse and other forms of mistreatment and exploitation of vulnerable persons.

The Pressure to Die

Second, even apparently free choices may be unduly influenced by the biases and wishes of others. Legalization proposals generally leave in place the laws against assisting most people to commit suicide, but they define a class of people whose suicides may be facilitated rather than prevented. That class typically includes people expected to live less than six months. Such predictions of a short life are notoriously unreliable. They also carry a built-in ambiguity, as some legal definitions of terminal illness include individuals who have a short time to live only if they do *not* receive life-supporting treatment. Thus, many people with chronic illnesses or disabilities—who could live a long time if they receive basic care—may be swept up in such a definition. However wide or narrow the category may be, it defines a group of people whose death by lethal overdose is wrongly treated by the law as objectively good or acceptable, unlike the suicide of anyone else.

By rescinding legal protection for the lives of one group of people, the government implicitly communicates the message—before anyone signs a form to accept this alleged benefit—that they may be better off dead. Thus, the bias of too many able-bodied people against the value of life for someone with an illness or disability is embodied in official policy.

This biased judgment is fueled by the excessively high premium our culture places on productivity and autonomy, which tends to discount the lives of those who have a disability or are dependent on others. If these persons say they want to die, others may be tempted to regard this not as a call for help but as the reasonable response to what they agree is a meaningless life. Those who choose to live may then be seen as selfish or irrational, as a needless burden on others, and even be encouraged to view themselves that way.

In short, the assisted-suicide agenda promotes a narrow and distorted notion of freedom, by creating an *expectation* that certain people, unlike others, will be served by being helped to choose death. Many people with illnesses and disabilities who struggle against great odds for their genuine rights—the right to adequate health care and housing, opportunities for work and mobility, and so on—are deservedly suspicious when the freedom society most eagerly offers them is the "freedom" to take their lives.

The Right to Life

Third, there is a more profound reason why the campaign for assisted suicide is a threat, not an aid, to authentic human freedom.

The founders of our country declared that each human being has certain inalienable rights that government must protect. It is no accident that they named life before liberty and the pursuit of happiness. Life itself is a basic human good, the condition for enjoying all other goods on this earth. Therefore the right to life is the most basic human right. Other valued rights—the right to vote, to freedom of speech, or to equal protection under law—lose their foundation if life itself can be destroyed with impunity.

As Christians, we go even further: Life is our first gift from an infinitely loving Creator. It is the most fundamental element of our God-given human dignity. Moreover, by assuming and sharing our human nature, the Son of God has more fully revealed and enhanced the sacred character of each human life.

Therefore, one cannot uphold human freedom and dignity by devaluing human life. A choice to take one's life is a supreme contradiction of freedom, a choice to eliminate all choices. And a society that devalues some people's lives, by hastening and facilitating their deaths, will ultimately lose respect for their other rights and freedoms.

Thus, in countries that have used the idea of personal autonomy to justify voluntary assisted suicide and euthanasia, physicians have moved on to take the lives of adults who never asked to die, and newborn children who have no choice in the matter. They have developed their own concept of a "life not worth living" that has little to do with the choice of the patient. Leaders of the "aid in dying" movement in our country have also voiced support for ending the lives of people who never asked for death, whose lives *they* see as meaningless or as a costly burden on the community.

A False Compassion

The idea that assisting a suicide shows compassion and eliminates suffering is equally misguided. It eliminates the person, and results in suffering for those left behind—grieving families and friends, and other vulnerable people who may be influenced by this event to see death as an escape.

The sufferings caused by chronic or terminal illness are often severe. They cry out for our compassion, a word whose root meaning is to "suffer with" another person. True compassion alleviates suffering while maintaining solidarity with those who suffer. It does not put lethal drugs in their hands and abandon them to their suicidal impulses, or to the self-serving motives of others who may want them dead. It helps vulnerable people with their problems instead of treating them as the problem.

Taking life in the name of compassion also invites a slippery slope toward ending the lives of people with nonterminal conditions. Dutch doctors, who once limited euthanasia to terminally ill patients, now provide lethal drugs to people with chronic illnesses and disabilities, mental illness, and even melancholy. Once they convinced themselves that ending a short life can be an act of compassion, it was morbidly logical to conclude that ending a longer life may show even more compassion. Psychologically, as well, the physician who has begun to offer death as a solution for some illnesses is tempted to view it as the answer for an ever-broader range of problems.

This agenda actually risks adding to the suffering of seriously ill people. Their worst suffering is often not physical pain, which can be alleviated with competent medical care, but feelings of isolation and hopelessness. The realization that others—or society as a whole—may see their death as an acceptable or even desirable solution to their problems can only magnify this kind of suffering.

Even health care providers' ability and willingness to provide palliative care such as effective pain management can be undermined by authorizing assisted suicide. Studies indicate that untreated pain among terminally ill patients may increase and development of hospice care can stagnate after assisted suicide is legalized. Government programs and private insurers may even limit support for care that could extend life, while emphasizing the "cost-effective" solution of a doctor-prescribed death. The reason for such trends is easy to understand. Why would medical professionals spend a lifetime developing the empathy and skills needed for the difficult but important task of providing optimum care, once society has authorized a "solution" for suffering patients that requires no skill at all? Once some people have become candidates for the inexpensive treatment of assisted suicide, public and private payers for health coverage also find it easy to direct life-affirming resources elsewhere.

A Better Way

There is an infinitely better way to address the needs of people with serious illnesses.

Our society should embrace what Pope John Paul II called "the way of love and true mercy"—a readiness to surround patients with love, support, and companionship, providing the assistance needed to ease their physical, emotional, and spiritual suffering. This approach must be anchored in unconditional respect for their human dignity, beginning with respect for the inherent value of their lives.

Respect for life does not demand that we attempt to prolong life by using medical treatments that are ineffective or unduly burdensome. Nor does it mean we should deprive suffering patients of needed pain medications out of a misplaced or exaggerated fear that they might have the side effect of shortening life. The risk of such an effect is extremely low when pain medication is adjusted to a patient's level of pain, with the laudable purpose of simply addressing that pain. In fact, severe pain can shorten life, while effective palliative care can enhance the length as well as the quality of a person's life. It can even alleviate the fears and problems that lead some patients to the desperation of considering suicide.

Effective palliative care also allows patients to devote their attention to the unfinished business of their lives, to arrive at a sense of peace with God, with loved ones, and with themselves. No one should dismiss this time as useless or meaningless. Learning how to face this last stage of our earthly lives is one of the most important and meaningful things each of us will do, and caregivers who help people through this process are also doing enormously important work. As Christians, we believe that even suffering itself need not be meaningless—for as Pope John Paul II showed during his final illness, suffering accepted in love can bring us closer to the mystery of Christ's sacrifice for the salvation of others.

Protecting the Gift of Life

Catholics should be leaders in the effort to defend and uphold the principle that each of us has a right to *live* with dignity through every day of our lives. As disciples of one who is Lord of the living, we need to be messengers of the Gospel of Life. We should join with other concerned Americans, including disability rights advocates, charitable organizations, and members of the healing professions, to stand for the dignity of people with serious illnesses and disabilities and promote life-affirming solutions for their problems and hardships. We should ensure that the families of people with chronic or terminal illness will advocate for the rights of their loved ones, and will never feel they have been left alone in caring for their needs. The claim that the "quick fix" of an overdose of drugs can substitute for these efforts is an affront to patients, caregivers and the ideals of medicine.

When we grow old or sick and we are tempted to lose heart, we should be surrounded by people who ask, "How can we help?" We deserve to grow old in a society that views our cares and needs with a compassion grounded in respect, offering genuine support in our final days. The choices we make together now will decide whether this is the kind of caring society we will leave to future generations. We can help build a world in which love is stronger than death.

| "The consideration of euthanasia by a society that cannot provide adequate care to its most vulnerable members should be seen as an indictment of that society."

Legalizing Euthanasia Can Become a Slippery Slope

Sherif Emil

Sherif Emil is a pediatric surgeon at the Montreal Children's Hospital. In the following viewpoint, he maintains that a society that legalizes euthanasia is not a compassionate society. Emil worries that in his home province of Quebec, Canada, problems with the health care system have led to a loss of humanity and a growing belief that patients are a burden to the system. He points out that once euthanasia is legalized and accepted in Western societies, more and more patients, families, and medical professionals will turn to the option of euthanasia to relieve unbearable suffering. It will also be considered for conditions other than terminal illness. That is the situation, he suggests, in Belgium, where euthanasia was legalized years ago. He argues that there is a better alternative: palliative care, which relieves pain and provides support to terminally ill patients in their final days.

As you read, consider the following questions:

1. What province does the author claim fared the worst in a national survey of Canadians' attitudes, beliefs, and experiences with their own health care system?

2. According to the viewpoint, what is the legal age of consent in Quebec?

3. According to Emil, what controversial procedure does Quebec have the highest rate of in North America?

At the entry to Paris's oldest hospital, the Hôtel-Dieu, are these words: "To cure occasionally, to relieve often, to comfort always."

Medical historians ascribe this aphorism to Hippocrates, who also gave us our medical oath, an important principle of which is to not kill. And yet a culture of death, frequently disguised as the concept of "dying with dignity," is creeping into society and becoming increasingly sanctioned by politicians and the medical establishment.

A National Assembly committee held public hearings in 2010–11 and concluded that euthanasia, euphemistically called "medical aid in dying," should be legal in Quebec. This conclusion came in spite of the fact that two-thirds of the citizens who made presentations to the committee, including myself and many physicians, were opposed to euthanasia.

This week [in January 2013], spurred by a report from a panel of legal experts recommending that terminally ill adult patients be given the right to doctor-assisted suicide, the Quebec government said it will introduce legislation to that effect.

The Quebec Health Care Challenges

Nowhere is euthanasia more dangerous than here in Quebec. In 2010, the Canadian Medical Association published sobering results of a national survey of Canadians' attitudes, beliefs and experiences with their health care system. A large majority of

Canadians in every province concluded that the system is broken; but Quebec fared the worst.

As a pediatric surgeon in Montreal, I practise in an environment of constant triage, with decisions every day regarding which patient needs to go first. We do not have enough operating room resources, intensive care unit beds, hospital beds, nurses—and the list goes on. And we are the lucky ones, because we treat children; more resources are available to us than to those who treat adult patients. The situation for my counterparts who treat adults is far worse.

I have experienced the Quebec health care system over a quarter of a century, first as a medical student in the late 1980s, then as a pediatric-surgical trainee in the late 1990s, and now as a staff pediatric surgeon for the last four years. After I graduated from McGill [University], I went back to my native California to start my residency, carrying a tremendous pride in the education I had received and holding the environment that I had been trained in as a model for humane and compassionate health care.

Unfortunately, since I have moved back, I have come to learn through my observations as a physician and my experiences as a patient, as well as through being a friend and relative to many patients, that health care in Quebec is in deep crisis. The denial of this crisis by politicians and health care leaders does not make it any less severe.

A Crisis

The humanity of the health care system has all but disappeared over the past 25 years. The patient has come to be seen as a burden to the system, rather than the reason for its existence. The resource limitations and senseless governmental macro-management have destroyed the morale of many who are entrusted to take care of the most vulnerable. The voices of those who want to raise awareness of this decay are often drowned, rather than listened to. Encouraging stories of truly

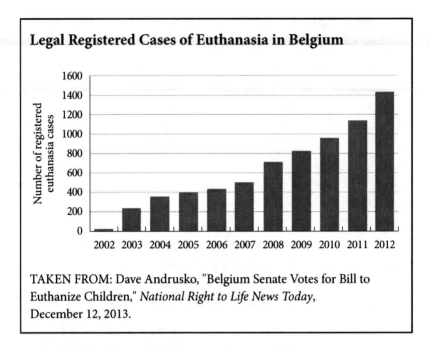

Legal Registered Cases of Euthanasia in Belgium

TAKEN FROM: Dave Andrusko, "Belgium Senate Votes for Bill to Euthanize Children," *National Right to Life News Today*, December 12, 2013.

patient- and family-centred care are now the exception, not the rule. Is this the type of environment in which we should introduce assisted suicide?

Imagine a patient in his or her final days in such a resource-limited, highly depersonalized system. The patient is requiring large amounts of resources to sustain life. His or her physicians and nurses know that death is imminent, and that it can be hastened by a lethal injection, allowing resources to go to patients who are seen as more worthy. How much dignity will that patient have if he or she chooses to cling to life?

Palliative Care

Is there a moral dimension to legalized killing? The three guiding principles of medicine are to do no harm, to support and sustain life, and to relieve suffering. It can be argued that legalized euthanasia is consistent with that third principle: relief of suffering. That would be true if there were no alternatives to relieve suffering. But there are, and Quebec has been a leader in this field through the work of palliative care pioneers like Dr. Balfour Mount and the many disciples who followed him. Palliative care is now available in the home and the hospice, allowing people to die with dignity in the presence of their families and loved ones. Pain medicine has matured into a specialty of its own, and billions of dollars have been invested into finding new treatments and methods to relieve pain and suffering. The armamentarium available to physicians has grown exponentially, and new medical journals are now exclusively dedicated to pain management and palliative care. When pain becomes an argument for ending life, it is the pain that must be killed, not the patient. Legalizing assisted suicide due to poorly treated or untreated pain is no different than legalizing assisted suicide due to poorly treated or untreated depression. It is no coincidence that Dr. Mount, as well as most of his colleagues in palliative care, stand firmly against euthanasia.

As a pediatric surgeon, I am particularly concerned about the fate of children under legalized euthanasia. In Quebec, the age of consent is 14—the youngest in North America. Will teenagers with terminal cancer or other diseases with a poor prognosis be able to choose to end their lives? Quebec has the highest elective-abortion rate in North America, and one of the highest in the Western world, despite the wide availability of birth control and sex education. It also has one of the highest pregnancy-termination rates for fetuses with congenital defects. Many of these defects are completely treatable, and are associated with excellent prognosis. It is legal in Quebec to terminate a pregnancy, even in the last trimester, when a congenital anomaly is identified. The fetus, who at that point may very well survive birth, is first killed and then delivered. What if parents discover these anomalies after birth, as sometimes occurs? Will they have the legal right to end their newborn's life?

The Slippery Slope

The slippery slope is closer than we think. We only have to look at the model the Quebec government is using for its policies on euthanasia: Belgium. Recently Dr. Catherine Dopchie, a Belgian oncologist and director of a palliative care unit, visited Quebec and spoke to large audiences in Montreal and Quebec City. She described the Pandora's box that was opened when euthanasia was legalized in Belgium 10 years ago. Out of fear of uncontrolled pain, many patients, their families and physicians don't even attempt palliative care, and rush toward physician-inflicted death instead, she reported. The field of palliative care is thus compromised; its practitioners having to fight to propose their services to patients before they jump onto the euthanasia bandwagon. A choice for euthanasia becomes the "courageous" thing to do, and subtle or not-so-subtle coercion to make that choice is omnipresent among the elderly and terminally ill, Dr. Dopchie said. What was originally proposed as a solution for extreme cases has become a well-marketed "therapeutic option."

After her departure from Montreal, we learned that doctors at University Hospital Brussels had euthanized twin brothers, 45 years old, who said they wanted to die because they had been told they were soon to go blind.

The consideration of euthanasia by a society that cannot provide adequate care to its most vulnerable members should be seen as an indictment of that society. Euthanasia is the easier choice for society to make. Mending a broken health care system that often does not dignify life, long before its end, is the more difficult choice, the one that requires honesty and leadership.

Even with the most advanced medical care, we can still cure occasionally but comfort always. I do not want to practise in a health care system where we kill occasionally and comfort rarely. For that reason, I have joined other Quebec physicians in a "total refusal of euthanasia" position. You can find out more about our position at caringalways.com.

> "It's easy to think doctors should have the legal right to prescribe a lethal dose of sedatives so that, when the time comes, [patients] can die at home, without pain, surrounded by loved ones."

There Is No Evidence That Legalizing Euthanasia Will Lead to a Slippery Slope

Dan Gardner

Dan Gardner is a journalist, author, blogger, and lecturer. In the following viewpoint, he rejects the claim that legalizing euthanasia will lead to a slippery slope. Gardner turns to the Dutch experience with legalized euthanasia that shows the rate of euthanasia as a percentage of total deaths in the country has actually decreased in recent years. He cites research that finds that most patients who chose euthanasia would have died within days, which sets to rest the accusation that the practice will spread from terminally ill patients to healthy people. Dutch research also shows that vulnerable segments of the population—the poor, the elderly, the disabled, minorities, and those with psychiatric

illness or depression—were not being pressured to choose eutha-
nasia to end their lives. Gardner argues that these facts should
help people make informed decisions on the legalization of eu-
thanasia instead of decisions being influenced by misinforma-
tion.

As you read, consider the following questions:

1. According to Gardner, in what year did the Netherlands legalize euthanasia?

2. According to a 2001 survey of physicians in the Netherlands and five other European countries, in how many countries were there reported incidents of the deliberate hastening of death?

3. What was the rate of euthanasia in the Netherlands in 2005, according to a Dutch study?

With the release of an important new report, and the launch of another charter [Canadian Charter of Rights and Freedom] challenge, the debate about euthanasia is flaring up again. It will be passionate. You will hear emotional claims from both sides. Many people will listen to nothing else. But for those who want to be rational, those who want to learn as much as they can and draw a conclusion based on evidence, there is one essential fact to bear in mind.

The Dutch are more honest than we are. Remember that.

If you've read anything about euthanasia, pro or con, chances are you have seen references to the Netherlands. And for good reason. The Dutch effectively legalized euthanasia in the early 1980s, and formally legalized it in 2002. Other countries—and two American states—have done the same, but the Dutch have had the most experience.

And that matters because the key argument against permitting euthanasia is the "slippery slope."

The Slippery Slope

Yes, opponents of euthanasia say. There are articulate, intelligent and thoughtful people, afflicted with terminal diseases, who say they want to decide when and how they will die. It's easy to be sympathetic. It's easy to think doctors should have the legal right to prescribe a lethal dose of sedatives so that, when the time comes, [patients] can die at home, without pain, surrounded by loved ones. It's even easy to think doctors should be able to inject them, if they are physically incapable of taking the overdose themselves.

But it won't stop there, they say. If we permit that, we will slide down a slippery slope.

What about people who aren't terminally stricken? What about the depressed and the mentally ill? What about elderly patients pressured by relatives who want to be relieved of the burden of their care? What about the mentally incompetent, who cannot consent? What about the disabled?

Every act of euthanasia will cheapen the value we put on life, they say. Every advance will make the next advance easier. Where will it end? Opponents of euthanasia are nothing if not passionate. They often conclude their arguments with references to the Nazis' murder of the disabled and other "undesirables." That's where it will end, they say.

If this is true, and the Dutch have had de facto legalized euthanasia for more than a quarter century, the Netherlands must be well down that slippery slope by now.

So they are, claim opponents of euthanasia. "By 1995, almost three per cent of all deaths were the result of euthanasia or assisted suicide," wrote Barbara Kay in the *National Post*, and there were hundreds of cases in which "doctors had acted without the consent of the patient, mainly for reasons of dementia."

That's the sort of claim you will see more of. Which is why you have to remember: The Dutch are more honest than we are.

False Assumptions

Notice what Kay simply assumes? What she implicitly leads the reader to conclude? That there was no euthanasia in the Netherlands before it was legalized. She makes the same assumption about Canada and other countries that now forbid it. Euthanasia? Here? Impossible. It's forbidden.

But it happens. All the time. A 2001 survey of physicians in the Netherlands and five other European countries, including four that banned euthanasia, found that the deliberate hastening of death in some form—whether euthanasia (prescribing drugs for someone to end their own life), physician-assisted suicide (the doctor injects the drugs), or ending life without explicit patient consent—occurred in every country. Granted, the reported Dutch rate of euthanasia (2.6 per cent) was higher than the rate in the other countries (which ranged from a low of zero in Italy to a high of 0.3 per cent in Belgium). But the rate at which lives were ended without explicit patient request was roughly the same in the Netherlands (0.7 per cent) as elsewhere (ranging from 0.1 per cent to 1.5 per cent).

And yes, it happens here, too. "Assisted dying presently goes on in various medical contexts in Canada," concluded the report of an expert panel convened by the Royal Society of Canada (RSC), released this week [in November 2011]. But we're not as honest as the Dutch. We won't say it's happening. We won't say it will continue to happen whether the law permits it or not. And we certainly won't talk about how to control and regulate it. No, we prefer to have a law forbidding euthanasia and simply pretend it doesn't happen.

Of course, as a consequence of that hypocrisy, critical decisions about end-of-life care are made in private, quietly, by the people involved. And this inflicts "anxiety, uncertainty, and needless suffering" on everyone, as the Royal Society of Canada report noted. And it means that end-of-life decisions "are gov-

Euthanasia in Canada

In June 2005 Francine Lalonde—one of [the Canadian] Parliament's most vocal advocates of legalizing assisted suicide—introduced Bill C-407, which would have drastically amended existing legislation by permitting assisted suicide under sanctioned conditions. The bill's passing was impeded by elections in 2006 and 2008; but in May 2009, Lalonde introduced another bill, Bill C-384, an almost identical version but with slight revisions.

After much debate in the House of Commons, the bill died upon its second reading on April 21, 2010, with a failed vote of 59 to 228. The vote demonstrated how politicians remain extremely divided on this issue. Nearly every member of the Bloc Québécois supported the legislation, along with one independent and a small number of Liberal, New Democratic, and Conservative members of Parliament. Today, euthanasia remains a contentious issue of debate in Canadian society and politics.

"Euthanasia in Canada," Gale Canada in Context, 2011.

erned by arbitrariness and lack of clarity rather than transparent, democratically enacted norms."

But an awful lot of Canadians prefer that to being honest.

The Dutch Advantage

Fortunately, the Dutch are blessed with a far more open social and political culture. It's also a more pragmatic culture. The Dutch frankly acknowledge the existence of difficult problems and they don't try to do what cannot be done. This honesty and practicality—not liberal anything-goes permissiveness—is the source of their drug and prostitution policies. It's also the reason why the Dutch legalized and regulated euthanasia. And why they rigorously studied the results.

In the first Dutch study, conducted in 1990, the rate of voluntary euthanasia was 1.7 per cent of all deaths. In 1995, it was 2.4 per cent. In 2000, it was 2.6 per cent. In 2005, the most recent year for which data are now available, the rate was 1.7 per cent—exactly the same as it was in 1990.

The rate of assisted suicide was 0.2 per cent in 1990. In 2005, it was 0.1 per cent.

The rate of "life-terminating acts without explicit request of the patient" was 0.8 per cent in 1990. In 2005, it was down by half to 0.4 per cent.

The research also showed that most patients who choose euthanasia would have died soon anyway: Almost half had a life expectancy of less than a week; only 8 per cent had a life expectancy of more than a month. As for those cases of "life-terminating acts without explicit request of the patient," the RSC report notes they "typically involve patients who are very close to death and are presently incompetent but where there has been an earlier discussion about hastening death with them and/or their relatives."

And, no, the vulnerable are not being singled out. A 2009 summary of research by Dutch scientists concluded "there is no evidence for a higher frequency of euthanasia among the elderly, people with low educational status, the poor, the physically disabled or chronically ill, minors, people with psychiatric illnesses including depression, or racial and ethnic minorities, compared with background population."

In sum, there is "no evidence of a slippery slope." The RSC report came to the same conclusion.

That's good to know. And we know it thanks to the honesty of the Dutch.

"*Critical thinking says that people should have 100 percent control over their own decisions as long as those decisions don't violate the rights of others. This is fourth-grade logic our elected officials are apparently incapable of comprehending.*"

Legalizing Euthanasia Leads to a Stronger and More Compassionate Society

Steve Siebold

Steve Siebold is an author and political and social commentator. In the following viewpoint, he maintains that society would be in much better shape if we allowed human beings to have control over their own life and death, instead of allowing legislators and religious authorities to determine such matters. He points out that it is religious belief that proposes terminally ill people suffer in unbearable pain for no reason. Siebold argues that no one should be making public policy based on the Bible because today we know much about the body and how the world works than they did thousands of years ago. He is also resentful that religious authorities are able to impose their views of morality on the rest of society. For society to flourish, he believes that people must stand up and take charge of their own lives—and that involves throwing off the shackles of centuries-old religious dogma.

As you read, consider the following questions:

1. According to Siebold, why is the population divided over assisted suicide?

2. What does the Christian Apologetics and Research Ministry say about suicide?

3. Who does Siebold say is more informed about the world than the greatest scholars of the Iron Age and the authors of the Bible?

Identical twin brothers in Belgium were euthanized by doctors in what has sparked an international debate, because unlike most cases of assisted suicide, the brothers were not terminally ill. Both were deaf and recently learned they were going blind as well. So distraught that they would not be able to hear or see one another, they chose to end their lives together by assisted suicide, which is legal in Belgium.

Here in America, Montana, Oregon and Washington [as well as Vermont] are the only states that permit some form of assisted suicide. Deliberately killing someone, even if done humanely and by a medical professional, has divided the population largely in part because of religious reasons.

When faced with terminal illness and significant suffering, we don't have the legal right to end our pain. For animals, it's humane; for humans, it's a capital offense. Heroes like the late Dr. Jack Kevorkian were villainized and thrown in jail for helping people escape their suffering. The delusion is we don't own our own bodies and lives. Critical thinking says that

Jack Kevorkian

Dr. Jack Kevorkian considered himself an angel of mercy, but his detractors dubbed him "Dr. Death." He was the inventor of a controversial suicide machine, which he used on June 4, 1990, to help end the life of a 54-year-old woman who had been in the early stages of Alzheimer's disease. His action raised a storm of debate over the rights of patients to choose the moment of death, and over what role doctors should play in that decision. . . .

During the 1990s, Kevorkian repeatedly staged assisted suicides and claimed he helped more than 130 people die. Kevorkian faced trial four times on charges of assisted suicide, but three of the trials resulted in acquittals and one was declared a mistrial. In March of 1999, Kevorkian faced trial for murder charges in the death of Thomas Youk, who was dying of Lou Gehrig's disease [amyotrophic lateral sclerosis (ALS)]. Because Youk could not administer lethal drugs to himself, Kevorkian did so. He documented the death on video and gave the tape to the television show *60 Minutes*. The jury found Kevorkian guilty of second-degree murder, and he was sentenced to 10–25 years in prison. He spent eight years in prison and was paroled in June of 2007 after promising not to assist in any more suicides.

"Jack Kevorkian,"
Gale Biography in Context, 2011.

people should have 100 percent control over their own decisions as long as those decisions don't violate the rights of others. This is fourth-grade logic our elected officials are apparently incapable of comprehending.

The Role of Religion

In the Roman Catholic Church, suicide is a sin, because only God has the authority to end a human life. No evidence exists to support this claim, yet it's the undercurrent of the laws banning assisted suicide. The Christian Apologetics and Research Ministry (CARM) says this: "God is the sovereign Lord who determines the day we die. Therefore, we are not to undermine God's authority."

Once again, we have religious leaders and organizations telling us what God wants with no proof to support their statements. Make no mistake: This is not about what God wants. This is religious zealotry masquerading as morality. This is about controlling society, and it works on the masses. The problem is once critical thinking is injected into the equation, this mass manipulation becomes obvious.

Here's my critical thinking question on this bold statement from the Catholic Church: "How do they know?" The church, Catholic or any other, has no more information than you or I do. Years ago they did, and that's where the manipulation began. People didn't have access to information and were largely ignorant and terrified to challenge the church. Those days are gone. Today, Americans are armed with more information and education at their fingertips than all the generations that preceded us combined. It's easy to scare an uneducated, ignorant populous, but once the playing field of education, knowledge and awareness is leveled, everything changes.

Educated people cannot be bullied or brainwashed. In the Information Age, you better have extraordinary evidence to support extraordinary claims, and religion offers no such evidence. The case made by the religious right against assisted suicide is based on a book written by relatively ignorant men. Today, a 12-year-old knows more about the world than the greatest scholars of the Iron Age and the authors of the Bible. The leap of faith that Christianity demands is that the Bible was inspired, and therefore written, by God himself. Again, not a shred of evidence exists to prove this claim, yet it has convinced 2 billion otherwise intelligent people that their book was written by a supernatural, omniscient being, even though it is filled with 1st-century ignorance. The idea that a merciful God is against ending human suffering is a prime example. It defies even a child's logic, yet it's ferociously observed and defiantly defended by most Americans.

Time for Critical Thinking

It's time for thinking people to stand up and start pushing back on issues that involve human suffering. If someone chooses to believe that God wants her to suffer through a terminal illness that's her decision, but when you force the rest of us to obey laws based on evidence-less beliefs, it's wrong and needs to be stopped. You're welcome to believe in Santa Claus, but when you outlaw burning wood in my fireplace so he can slide down the chimney you're going to have to prove he actually exists. Your faith is yours, not anyone else's. Forcing critical thinkers to adhere to laws based on fairy tales is wrong.

Unfortunately, the church isn't the only powerful group of people protesting assisted suicide. There are many physicians who are banding together to fight physician-assisted suicide as well. Once again, here's another powerful group of people who used to have far more clout in society than they have now, due to education and information available to the masses. Critical thinking on this is simple: If a physician-assisted suicide violates the individual physician's belief system, he shouldn't be forced to perform this service. For physicians who believe it's the right thing to do, they should be able to do it.

This whole argument boils down to a simple premise: Who is in charge of our lives? Doctors? Politicians? Religious leaders? Or us? Are we so feebleminded that we cannot be trusted to be responsible for our own existence? The answer is obviously no, yet that's exactly what the people in power would have us believe. They brainwash us to believe we need their laws, dogma and leadership to live our lives so they can exert their control.

When will Americans grow up emotionally and accept the fact that this is the one and only life we have evidence of that exists, and we should be allowed to live it on our own terms? The states have the power to allow and regulate assisted suicide or to prohibit it, and with enough pressure from critical thinkers we will someday have the freedom to end our lives with dignity. If enough critical thinkers band together, someday we'll be able to live and die on our own terms.

| "*Euthanasia is hardening from a medical option into an ideology.*"

Legalizing Euthanasia Has a Negative Impact on Society

Tom Mortier and Steven Bieseman

Tom Mortier and Steven Bieseman are teachers at Leuven University College in Belgium. In the following viewpoint, they assert that the legalization of euthanasia has drastically changed Belgian society in a number of ways. First, it has been a slippery slope; euthanasia is now being utilized by people with emotional issues, such as depression, or treatable conditions. Second, there is a euthanasia culture that celebrates the right to kill oneself and ignores the rights of family members. Mortier and Bieseman observe that anyone who questions this culture is marginalized and regarded as rigid and heartless. Finally, they worry that euthanasia has loosened the bonds that hold society together, and that the emphasis on self-determination has damaged Belgium's sense of community and compassion for the vulnerable of society.

As you read, consider the following questions:

1. According to the authors, in what year did Belgium legalize euthanasia?

2. How do the authors say that euthanasia is being promoted in Belgium?

3. According to the viewpoint, what Belgium philosopher
is a strong opponent of euthanasia?

In 2002, Belgium became the second country in the world
after its neighbour, the Netherlands, to legalise euthanasia.
Over the next decade, our country has become a living labo-
ratory for radical social change. With many other countries
debating legalisation at the moment, now is a good moment
to stand back and take a good long look at the results.

Belgian Politics

In 2002 Belgium was governed by a coalition of Liberals, So-
cialists and the Green party. The slightly more conservative
Christian Democrats had been excluded. With blue as the co-
lour of the Liberals and red of the left-leaning Social Democrats, the press dubbed it the purple coalition.

The Christian Democrats took a dim view of euthanasia,
but they were in opposition. The purple coalition was free to
pass a euthanasia law based on the view that an individual
should always have a "free choice" to end his life. In absolutiz-
ing individual self-determination, the left and the right found
common ground.

The law states that doctors can help patients to die when
they freely express a wish to die because they are suffering in-
tractable and unbearable pain. The patient needs to consult a
second independent doctor; for nonterminal illnesses an independent psychiatrist must approve. In practice, however, this
independence is irrelevant. Belgium is a small country and
compliant doctors are easy to find.

Slippery Slope

A string of recent cases leaves no doubt that the euthanasia
law has fundamentally and drastically changed Belgian society.
Last year [2012] 45-year-old deaf identical twin brothers, who

couldn't bear the thought of going blind, were granted euthanasia. Doctors granted their request because they "had nothing to live for" anyway. According to the doctor who gave the lethal injection, it was not "such a big deal".

In another case, a 44-year-old woman with chronic anorexia nervosa was euthanised. Then a 64-year-old woman suffering from chronic depression was euthanised without informing her relatives. The doctors defended their decisions by explaining that these extreme and exceptional cases were legitimate because all legal conditions were met.

Euthanasia is hardening from a medical option into an ideology. Belgium's euthanasia doctors even believe they are being humane because they are liberating people from their misery. Fundamentalist humanists go further and describe euthanasia as the ultimate act of self-determination. The opinion of the patient's family has no weight whatsoever. A doctor is entitled to give the mother of a family a lethal injection without offering any explanation to her children. Euthanasia is being promoted as a "beautiful" and positive way to die. Doctors are transplanting organs from patients who die in the operation. (This is said to make their lives meaningful.) The law may soon allow children and patients with dementia to be euthanised.

Opposition to Euthanasia in Belgium

Since 2002 opponents of the law (like us) have been marginalised as rigid and heartless conservatives who feel ill at ease in a postmodern, pluralistic and progressive society like Belgium. The Christian Democrats have repudiated their traditional values and support the law. Questioning it has become taboo because the absolute right of the individual might be violated.

There are still some significant critics, apart from the Catholic Church. The Belgian philosopher Herman De Dijn is an outspoken opponent. He describes Belgium as a "sentimentalist society" in which traditional values have been drastically minimized and replaced by subjective preferences. A sentimentalist society no longer subscribes to ethical values other than those which are related to the search for individual happiness (autonomy and no harm). Communal responsibilities and moral institutions are being discarded in the search for purely individual well-being; interdependence and connectedness are ignored.

De Dijn feels that this is the nub of the problem. A human being is not a bundle of individual feelings, opinions and preferences, but part of a species, a member of mankind, a vital link in the moral ecology where every individual has a unique symbolic value. Respect for human dignity includes not only respect for personal choices but also for connectedness to loved ones and society.

Supporters of the euthanasia regime repudiate this secular critique—as well as the baneful influence of the Catholic Church. However, their ideology of absolute self-determination has become so strong that it is morphing into a theology, a quasi-religious fanaticism. They have invented comforting symbols and rituals to express their beliefs. A self-determination card describes a patient's final wishes so that the social services know what to do in a terminal illness. There are centres where people can ask questions about how euthanasia can be performed. There is indoctrination in self-determination for doctors and volunteers who wear their euthanasia-enabler certificates as badges of honour.

The Threat to Humanism

Nonetheless, we are hopeful. Surely it must be possible to convince the Belgian public that something is terribly, terribly wrong when politicians are debating whether parents can legally have their children put down. It is not humane and it is not scientific. There is no scientific scale of unbearable suffering. With advances in pain relief, euthanasia is not even needed.

The key insight of the green movement is that all living beings are interconnected—even us humans. Especially us humans. The job of politicians is to protect this connectedness. Otherwise, why should parents care for their dependent children? Why should children care for dependent parents? Once we lose the sense that each of us is bound to one another with invisible cords of fellowship, we will end by killing all those who are burdens on society. And at some stage, all of us are going to be burdens.

Euthanasia does not threaten religious dogmas. Churches will stay open no matter what happens in hospitals and nursing homes. What is threatened is humanism. Instead of standing strong, arms linked together as brothers and sisters, the dogma of self-determination separates us, places us in bubbles of isolation, and then offers to kill us—if we want. In today's Belgium, all of us are at risk.

Periodical and Internet Sources Bibliography

The following articles have been selected to supplement the diverse views presented in this chapter.

JoNel Aleccia	"Doctor-Assisted Death: A Dad's Choice Sheds Light on National Issue," NBC News, April 10, 2013.
Sarah Boseley	"Assisted Dying: 'I've Had a Good Life, Now I Am Planning for a Good Death,'" *Guardian* (UK), July 9, 2013.
Lewis M. Cohen	"Deaths with Dignity," *Slate*, June 6, 2013.
Erik Eckholm	"'Aid in Dying' Movement Takes Hold in Some States," *New York Times*, February 7, 2014.
Serena Gordon	"Physician-Assisted Suicide Program Rarely Used, Study Finds," HealthDay, April 10, 2013.
Dan Kadlec	"A Good Death: How Boomers Will Change the World a Final Time," *Time*, August 14, 2013.
Robert Leeson	"Euthanasia Can Be an Economic Decision Made Early," SFGate.com, October 11, 2013.
Daniel Miller	"My Life Is Miserable, Demeaning and Undignified Says Locked-In Syndrome Sufferer as He Asks High Court Judges to Give Him the Right to Die," *Daily Mail* (UK), June 19, 2012.
Sam Smith	"Society Needs to Make a Choice on Physician-Assisted Suicide, Doctors of BC Say," *Metro* (Canada), April 8, 2014.
Peter Ubel	"Death with Dignity Should Not Be Equated with Physician Assisted Suicide," *Forbes*, August 26, 2013.

CHAPTER 3

What Controversies Impact the Euthanasia Debate?

Chapter Preface

On September 30, 2013, a forty-four-year-old Belgian man named Nathan Verhelst became one of the thousands of Belgians who have taken advantage of the nation's euthanasia law since the process was legalized in 2002. The vast majority of euthanasia applications are made by people with incurable diseases who have no chance of recovery and are living with unbearable physical pain. The quality of life for many of these patients is very poor, as they struggle to survive, maintain their dignity, and find meaning and pleasure from life while dealing with intolerable pain.

However, Nathan Verhelst's situation was very different from the majority of euthanasia cases in Belgium. His situation was so unique, in fact, and raised so many complicated questions about the issue of euthanasia, that his death made international news.

Verhelst was born female in Belgium and grew up feeling that he was a boy trapped in a girl's body. He was "the girl that nobody wanted," as he was quoted as saying in the *Christian Post*. He continued, "While my brothers were celebrated, I got a storage room above the garage as a bedroom. 'If only you had been a boy,' my mother complained. I was tolerated, nothing more."

In 2009 Verhelst began taking steps toward gender reassignment surgery with hormone therapy. A few years later, he underwent several reassignment surgeries to complete his journey to physically become male. He underwent a mastectomy and had operations to construct a penis. When he examined himself in the mirror, however, he was disgusted with the results of the failed surgeries. Devastated, he no longer wanted to live.

Verhelst applied for medical euthanasia. His request was approved in late 2013. Physicians found that he was in unbearable psychological pain from his experiences and determined that his decision to end his life was not an impulsive one. In his case, qualified professionals found that his emotional suffering had been lifelong, unrelenting, and insufferable. On September 23, 2013, Verhelst hosted an intimate farewell party with friends and said his goodbyes. On September 30, he died by injection of a fatal dose of medications.

The nature of Verhelst's personal struggle and the tragic outcome of the case led many people to examine their own feelings about euthanasia, especially when it is used in cases of extreme emotional suffering. Many critics question whether euthanasia should even be used in cases of psychological suffering, such as with Verhelst. They wonder whether he could have been helped with intense psychological counseling. For many, euthanasia is not an ethical or moral solution to what could be a treatable problem.

The issue of whether patients with extreme psychological pain should be eligible for voluntary euthanasia is one of the topics explored in the following chapter, which examines controversies that impact the euthanasia debate.

"In the end, we are discussing people's lives when we discuss euthanasia. But the lives in question are ones in which there is much suffering."

Child Euthanasia Should Be Allowed

Luke J. Davies

Luke J. Davies is a philosophy graduate student at the University of Oxford in England. In the following viewpoint, he argues that it should be permissible to offer euthanasia to children suffering from unbearable pain as a result of a terminal illness. Davies contends that it is understandable for people to be concerned over such a policy, but ultimately there is no reason to prohibit it. One of the main objections to such a bill is that children do not have the mental capacity to fully comprehend the choice and to make such a profound decision. Davies argues that this assumption is wrong because children develop their critical and emotional capacities at different rates. Therefore, some children will have the capacity to make the decision, others won't—just like adults. If there are adequate safeguards and strict guidelines, he argues, it would ensure that only those children who have the capacity to make the decision can have the euthanasia option.

As you read, consider the following questions:

1. According to the author, what was the vote of the upper house of the Belgian Federal Parliament on the bill that legalizes euthanasia for children suffering from a terminal illness?

2. What kind of physical pain does the author find that the child must be in before euthanasia will be approved?

3. How long has euthanasia been legal in Belgium, as of 2014?

Last week [in January 2014] the upper house of the Belgian Federal Parliament voted (50 to 17) that euthanasia should be legal for children suffering from a terminal illness that is causing severe physical pain. The bill legalizing the practice requires that the child understand what euthanasia is, and that parents provide their written consent. Unlike the Netherlands, which allows euthanasia for children over the age of 12, there will be no minimum age in Belgium.

The passing of this bill, which has yet to be turned into a law, has been met with severe criticism in Belgium and abroad, mostly from religious and conservative groups. From what I have read, there are three main lines of argument against allowing euthanasia for children. The first maintains that allowing euthanasia for children is the first in a long series of steps that will lead to some Third Reich–like eugenics program. The second maintains that children do not have the capacity to make a decision to be euthanized. The third maintains that the legalization of euthanasia for children would lead to parents or health care professionals putting pressure on children to opt for that choice. I believe that each of these arguments fails to demonstrate that the bill should not pass, and will spend the remainder of this [viewpoint] explaining why.

Belgium's Child Euthanasia Law

On 13 February 2014, the Belgian [Federal] Parliament approved, by a vote of 86–44 with 12 abstentions, a bill extending the right of euthanasia to terminally ill children of any age. The "right to die" was legalized for adults in Belgium in 2002. The language of the bill, as reported by the BBC, would require the patient to be in unbearable physical pain and to make multiple requests to die. The request would require the approval of the parents or guardians, the patient's medical team, and psychiatrists. Public opinion appeared favorable, but pediatricians and the Catholic Church strongly opposed the measure, asserting that children have the right to palliative care and should not be permitted to make a choice of such gravity.

"Assisted Suicide and Euthanasia,"
Global Issues in Context Online Collection, 2014.

The Slippery Slope Argument

First, the worry that euthanasia being allowed for children will lead to a eugenics program is the result of the first draft of the bill, which included cases of depression, anorexia and other mental illnesses as valid reasons for the child's decision to die. The belief seems to be that the state should not be able to determine what makes a life worth living (and thus ending); for if it did, then it might begin to withhold lifesaving treatment from some in pursuit of an ethically indefensible ideal— i.e., one in which only those who fit a certain mold are allowed to live. Put simply, it is a 'slippery slope' style argument: If we allow doctors to help children die, this will lead to doctors choosing who gets to live.

There are two things (at least) to say in response to this. First, the bill has changed from its original form. As I have already mentioned, only physical pain that is constant, severe, and the result of an unbeatable illness will be sufficient for a child's being considered for euthanasia—assuming that he or she has met the other criteria. This means that there will be a narrower set of criteria for children than there is for adults. Second, the choice to make it legal for a medical professional to help someone who is suffering end his or her life, no matter the age of that person, is simply not the same as giving that professional the power to determine who receives lifesaving treatment.

Second, some believe that a child does not possess the capacity to make a decision to end his or her own life. Given that the choice to die must be the patient's own, the truth of that statement would constitute grounds for dismissing the bill.

I believe that this objection to the bill wrongly assumes that all children develop their critical and emotional capacities at the same rate, which is simply not true. It may be the case that the vast majority of children who are suffering from a terminal illness will be incapable to make the decision to die because they are unable to satisfy the criteria for understanding and appreciating the choice. Is this a reason for denying *all* children the right to make a choice? I think not. There will always be worries when we allow euthanasia that someone gets euthanised who didn't satisfy the criteria. This is no different with adults or children. However, I don't believe that this is an argument against the practice; it is merely an argument for making the criteria as clear as possible, and providing adequate training for the health care professionals who will be charged with carrying out the assessments. It is not clear to me that the criteria ought to include a minimum age requirement if what is required conceptually and emotionally from the person—child or adult—is sufficiently clear.

Undue Pressure

Finally, and most pressingly I believe, is the worry that undue pressure will befall any child who is, if consenting, a candidate for euthanasia. This worry is a result of the fact that doctors will be permitted to suggest euthanasia as an option for a child who suffers from a condition that qualifies them for the procedure. It is not difficult to believe that the child to whom this is suggested might feel some form of obligation to consent. Similar pressures, it is thought, might come from the parents. This is also a problem for euthanasia in general, not just for children. There can be a huge emotional and financial burden caused by prolonged and untreatable illness. If the family or doctor suggests euthanasia, the ill person may feel pressured to consent.

But, again, I believe this isn't an argument against the practice on the whole, but an argument for being careful. If it turned out that there was no way to avoid allowing people to die who didn't actually meet the criteria, then I would concede that euthanasia should not be permitted. However, I don't believe that the risk is that great, especially given that the practice has been legal in Belgium for the last 12 years.

In the end, we are discussing people's lives when we discuss euthanasia. But the lives in question are ones in which there is much suffering. At least in Belgium, adults are permitted to choose to end their life when that suffering is being caused by a condition that cannot be treated. I clearly side with those who believe that euthanasia is permissible—and might go further in thinking that its provision should be obligatory for those who want it. But the question in the Belgian case is not "Should we allow euthanasia?" That has already been settled. The question is, "If it is allowed for adults deemed to be competent to make the decision, why should it not be permitted for children who are also competent?" I for one cannot see a reason, but would be interested to hear more arguments to the contrary.

> *"Death, so far as we know, is terribly final. And if you're opting for death, you need to be sure that you've got it right."*

Euthanasia for Children Is Wrong—As Belgium Proposes New Law

Charles Foster

Charles Foster is a lawyer and research associate at the University of Oxford in England. In the following viewpoint, he outlines four dangerous misconceptions about euthanasia that make extending it to children a bad idea. First, modern palliative care can control unbearable suffering. Second, it is impossible for children to understand the complexity and finality of death to make a fully informed decision. Third, Foster worries that children might be pressured by physicians or family members to end their lives before they are ready. Fourth, there are other relevant parties involved, including family members and medical staff, and therefore the child does not have the right to self-determination when it comes to ending his or her life, Foster concludes.

As you read, consider the following questions:

1. According to the author, what three European countries permit adult euthanasia?

2. How does the author describe the process of passive euthanasia?

3. What does the author say that the Belgian law legalizing child euthanasia makes doctors?

Belgium is mooting an unprecedented law that would allow the voluntary euthanasia of children.

Voluntary euthanasia is intentionally ending a life at the request of the patient. It is lawful, on various differing grounds, in several jurisdictions, including Belgium, the Netherlands and Luxembourg.

In Belgium, the patient must be in a condition of constant and unbearable physical or psychological suffering resulting from a serious and incurable disorder caused by illness or accident, for which medical treatment is futile, and there must be no possibility of improvement. The patient must also be an adult.

But misconceptions about voluntary euthanasia make extending this to children a bad proposal. Here are four of them.

Euthanasia's the Only Way to End Suffering

This is untrue. Given modern palliative care (which is likely to be available in any European jurisdiction in which active euthanasia is proposed), there is simply no need for euthanasia. Pain and much-feared symptoms such as choking can all be controlled effectively.

Pro-euthanasists love stories about people going screaming to their deaths. The stories are out of date, and it is disingenuous or ignorant, as well as alarmist and unkind, to let people believe it's inevitable.

In the vanishingly rare cases of suffering that cannot be palliated using orthodox techniques, it is always possible to sedate the patient to unconsciousness and withdraw food and fluids (sometimes referred to as "passive euthanasia"). This leads to a painless death in a few days.

You could say that it is intellectually dishonest to cause death in this way and deny a quick death by lethal injection, but many feel that there is a distinction of great moral weight between causing death by an act (for example an injection) and causing death by omission. That distinction has proved its worth in the law of murder.

Children Can Make Informed Decisions

Let's suppose, for the sake of argument, that there are no good reasons why the law shouldn't permit the euthanasia of a fully capacious adult. (In fact there are some very good reasons: I touch on some of them below.) And if that is so, why shouldn't children be the beneficiaries of a similar compassionate law?

Death, so far as we know, is terribly final. And if you're opting for death, you need to be sure that you've got it right. This demands an understanding of many complex facts (such as prognosis—how your disease or condition is going to pan out—and your therapeutic and palliative options), and an evaluation of their significance. It's hard for anyone; it's likely to be impossible for children.

There's lots of evidence to show that when we find ourselves in the situations we have most feared (for instance severe disability), we find that those situations are nothing like as unbearable as we anticipated. When we are stripped of much, we value all the more what is left. Try explaining that to a child.

If children can't make an informed decision, perhaps also because they're simply too young or too ill, they can't be autonomous. Of course the decision makers will usually be well meaning, and will do their best to be well informed and objective, but it is hard to be honest about one's own motives.

Children Won't Be Pressurised into Death

The argument that someone might be pressurised to choose to die is commonly used when talking about older people or those with dementia (also being considered in Belgium) who might be seen as a "burden". For children, you might argue that they are less likely to be seen in this way. But children could easily think, or be actively or unconsciously persuaded, that they should opt for death because their illness causes trouble for their parents.

A Child Is the Only Relevant Decision Maker

The autonomy argument for adults goes: "It's my life and no one has the right to tell me what to do with it." This philosophy permeates and corrodes law and ethics because it doesn't accurately reflect the way the world is. We're relational entities. Everything I do affects someone. And in the context of the euthanasia of children, the following problems arise.

First, the death of a child (obviously) affects families, friends, carers and clinicians in many complex ways. The effects on others of my death ought to be factored into my decision to end my own life. Children won't be able to do that when deciding whether or not to end their own lives. This again falls into the idea of informed consent.

Second, someone's got to do the killing. That probably means doctors. If the law allows professional carers to become professional executioners, the medical profession will also be dangerously and irrevocably changed.

| "For most of us, the instinct to cling to life is so deep that helping another human being end it seems unthinkable."

Euthanasia Should Be Allowed for Emotional Suffering

Mary Elizabeth Williams

Mary Elizabeth Williams is an author and staff writer for Salon. In the following viewpoint, she recounts the tragic story of Nathan Verhelst, a Belgian transgender man who opted for euthanasia because of extreme and chronic emotional suffering. Williams admits that Verhelst's case is very troubling because for most people such an act is unimaginable unless they are in unbearable physical pain. Others worry about creating a culture of death in which life has little value and suicide becomes routine. Yet Williams argues that people in extreme emotional pain, such as Verhelst, are living a life that is unbearable to them. Many of these sufferers will end up committing suicide. Williams maintains that individuals in emotional turmoil should have the option of physician-assisted death, which first evaluates a person's state of mind and provides support to those seeking an end to life.

Mary Elizabeth Williams, "Euthanasia for Emotional Pain: Mercy or a 'Culture of Death?,'" Salon, October 7, 2013. This article first appeared in Salon.com, at http://www.Salon.com. An online version remains in the Salon archives. Reprinted with permission.

As you read, consider the following questions:

1. According to Williams, in Belgium in 2012 how many cases of euthanasia were attributed to psychological reasons?

2. In what year does the author report that Nathan Verhelst began the process of hormone and surgical transition?

3. What percentage of transgender Americans have attempted suicide, according to Williams?

"I was the girl no one wanted," Nathan Verhelst said. And then, a few hours later, Nathan Verhelst died. Earlier this month [in October 2013], the 44-year-old Brussels transgender man deliberately ended his life with a lethal cocktail of medication—and he did so with a doctor's assistance and his government's blessing. His death has raised ethical debates around the world.

As the BBC reported last month, Verhelst's case made relatively few headlines in Belgium, where euthanasia has been legal since 2002. In a process described as "serene and beautiful," a fatal dose of barbiturates is administered and the person usually dies "within 5 minutes." Though the Belgian evaluation commission for euthanasia says the majority of applicants for euthanasia are over age 60 and more than 75 percent have terminal cancer, individuals can also apply based on emotional suffering. The country reports there were 52 cases of euthanasia for psychological reasons last year.

Nathan Verhelst

In an interview with *Het Laatste Nieuws* before his death, Verhelst described growing up as a girl in an unloving family that had wished for a boy. A conversation with his mother in the same publication seems to confirm his assessment. "When I first saw 'Nancy,' my dream was shattered," she said. "She was

Key Facts About Depression

- Depression is a common mental disorder. Globally, more than 350 million people of all ages suffer from depression.

- Depression is the leading cause of disability worldwide, and is a major contributor to the global burden of disease.

- More women are affected by depression than men.

- At its worst, depression can lead to suicide.

- There are effective treatments for depression.

"Depression," World Health Organization, October 2012.

so ugly. I had a phantom birth. Her death does not bother me. . . . For me, this chapter closed. Her death does not bother me. I feel no sorrow, no doubt or remorse. We never had a bond which could therefore not be broken."

Verhelst began the process of hormone and surgical transition in 2009 but by last year was severely distressed at the results of a double mastectomy and penis surgery. "I was ready to celebrate my new birth," he said, "but when I looked in the mirror, I was disgusted with myself. My new breasts did not match my expectations and my penis had symptoms of rejection. I do not want to be a monster."

A Culture of Death?

The hospital where Verhelst died told the BBC that he met his end "in all serenity" after an "extremely rigorous procedure" of vetting. In Belgium, candidates must demonstrate a "voluntary, considered and repeated" desire to end life. University of

Antwerp professor Evelien Delbeke told the *Huffington Post* Saturday that "our legislation is pretty strict. A strict set of conditions needs to be met and several doctors are involved in each case." There is a waiting period, and at least two doctors must approve the procedure—three if the grounds are psychological rather than physical.

For most of us, the instinct to cling to life is so deep that helping another human being end it seems unthinkable. And so for us, the news of Verhelst's death—accompanied by reports of rising euthanasia rates in the three countries where it's legal (Luxembourg and the Netherlands are the others) sends an inevitable chill to the heart. Writing in the *Herald Sun* Sunday, Rita Panahi said that "what appears compassionate in theory can have sinister implications in practice. . . . We don't want to engender a culture that devalues the lives of the infirm, elderly, disabled or the clinically depressed. A culture where 'mercy killings' become the expected outcome for those considered a burden on society." In the *Telegraph*, Tim Stanley was even more concerned, stating, "Belgium and the Netherlands list 'death' among their accepted forms of medical therapy, performed with a chilling bureaucratic efficiency that has the effect of making it all appear perfectly normal and entirely routine. What was once forced upon people by authoritarian regimes is now becoming vogue by means of the ballot box. Societies are shuffling towards a culture of death."

Stanley is heartbreakingly correct when he writes that Verhelst "needed love." In the U.S., it's estimated that a "staggering" 41 percent of transgender individuals have attempted suicide, a figure that skyrockets even higher among transgender men and women who've been harassed or assaulted. Verhelst's history suggests a life that was marred by extreme mental pain, much of which could have been defused had he been treated with more understanding and compassion from the beginning. Bioethicist Arthur Caplan told NBC this week, "When you move away from the realm of terminal illness, toward judgments about suffering, you are starting down a very dangerous path and one that's extremely slippery"—and no one with a soul wants to build a world in which the already viciously marginalized are in any way made to feel that their lives are more expendable than others.

But if you've ever lost someone you loved to suicide, you know how very determined they can be. You know how real and profound their suffering is. When I think of a good friend who killed herself a few years ago, the one thing that gives me peace is the hope that in the end, she found a release from the mental torment that made her life unbearable. It's a state of mind few of us have experienced firsthand, and in a better, kinder world, we would be devoting more resources to the best intervention and medication for those at-risk individuals so that life doesn't become a terminal condition. But even in the best world, there are always going to be people for whom living is too painful. Verhelst needed love but maybe love was never going to be enough to save him. Suffering exists on a continuum, and it's impossible to gauge when it becomes unbearable for any individual—which is why these life and death choices are so hard to judge. For someone in extreme distress, though, how is the option of a razor to the wrist or a gun in the mouth more morally palatable than a physician-administered drug? And how is a mess left behind for a family member to find more compassionate than drifting off in a hospital bed?

"What was once forced upon people by
authoritarian regimes is now becoming
vogue by means of the ballot box."

Euthanasia Should Not Be Allowed for Emotional Suffering

Tim Stanley

Tim Stanley is an author, columnist, and blogger for the Tele-
graph. In the following viewpoint, he examines the sad and dis-
turbing case of Nathan Verhelst, a Belgian transgendered man
who was permitted to die by lethal injection when botched sex
change surgeries left him traumatized and depressed. Stanley
suggests that Verhelst needed love and human kindness, not the
help of the state to die. He reports that this is a trend in Bel-
gium, a country that seems to be undergoing a cultural shift on
the issue of death. Stanley asserts that Belgium has begun to
think of euthanasia as a legitimate solution for troubled indi-
viduals such as Verhelst. Instead, he argues, people suffering with
severe emotional pain should be offered love, spiritual guidance,
and human connection.

As you read, consider the following questions:

1. According to Stanley, euthanasia is the cause of one in how many deaths in Belgium?

2. What percentage of assisted deaths in Belgium does the author report go unreported?

3. What is the rate of assisted deaths in the Netherlands, according to Stanley?

Verhelst needed love, not help to die at the age of 44.

This week [in October 2013] Nathan Verhelst, only 44 years old, elected to be killed by lethal injection because he was left traumatised by a botched sex change operation. It's a story full of incredible pain: born into an identity he couldn't stand, abandoned by his mother, revolted by the body that doctors created for him and, finally, committing suicide with the help of the state. What's most tragic of all is how it ends. Nathan Verhelst was clearly a lonely man in desperate need of human sympathy and kindness. Yet that kindness came not in the form of love but a lethal injection. Is this the West's idea of humane behaviour?

This isn't a story about transgenderism. The change from becoming one sex to another is complex, risky and fraught with emotion—but a lot of people achieve the transition and are happy with the results. Whether or not Verhelst should have undergone the change is a matter between him and his doctors and worthy of little more comment than, "Good luck." No, this is a story about a man who went through a personal Hell that could have been sparked by any variety of emotional distress and who wound up hating himself, lonely and in-clined to give up living altogether. Aside from the personal tragedy involved, what gives the story a particular relevance for all of us is that the Belgian state regarded helping him to die as a legitimate response to his problems. And this is part of a growing trend.

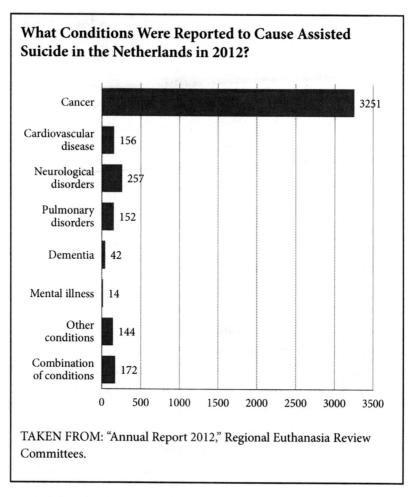

What Conditions Were Reported to Cause Assisted Suicide in the Netherlands in 2012?

Condition	Value
Cancer	3251
Cardiovascular disease	156
Neurological disorders	257
Pulmonary disorders	152
Dementia	42
Mental illness	14
Other conditions	144
Combination of conditions	172

TAKEN FROM: "Annual Report 2012," Regional Euthanasia Review Committees.

Belgian law states that citizens can be euthanised if a doctor confirms that they are in "constant and unbearable physical or psychological pain" resulting from an "accident or incurable illness". In the past year alone, the number of people electing to be killed jumped 25 per cent and it's now the cause of 1 in 50 deaths in the country. Recent cases have included a 44-year-old woman with chronic anorexia nervosa and a 64-year-old woman with chronic depression. Of course, there's a lot of data we don't know about. One survey found that 32 per cent of assisted deaths are conducted without request and 47 per cent go unreported. It's not unreasonable, then, to speculate that Belgian society is undergoing a slow cultural shift in the way that it regards death.

The Situation in the Netherlands

If you find that troubling, compare it with what's happening in the Netherlands. There, 1 in 30 deaths are now assisted. A private charity operates mobile euthanasia units, which travel from one care home to another—door-to-door—to help anyone to die who has been denied the opportunity by a doctor. They only visit each home once a week to relieve the potential psychological burden—but it must still be quite a shock when a group of smiling nurses turn up at your door and politely ask if you'd like to die today.

What science fiction writers of the past imagined as a fantastical reflection on the lack of humanity of their contemporary society has become concrete reality in ours. If you want, we can now kill you in an afternoon. Belgium and the Netherlands list "death" among their accepted forms of medical therapy, performed with a chilling bureaucratic efficiency that has the effect of making it all appear perfectly normal and entirely routine. What was once forced upon people by authoritarian regimes is now becoming vogue by means of the ballot box. Societies are shuffling towards a culture of death. Willingly.

Of course, defenders of euthanasia will insist that they are simply expanding individual freedom, that to live or die is the ultimate expression of free choice. Perhaps. But how do we balance that freedom with our responsibility to cherish life and support one another? Take the case of Nathan Verhelst. What is the morally superior response to his pain: to accept his misery as his own state of affairs and charitably give him a lethal injection? Or to reach out to a desperate lost soul, convince him that he is beautiful in the way that all human beings are beautiful, and plead with him to live with the assurance that he won't face his demons alone? Nathan Verhelst didn't "need" an assisted death—he needed love. It is to the shame of all of us that we failed to give it, offering him pointless annihilation instead.

> "Perhaps it takes the dramatic actions of a flawed advocate like Dr. Jack Kevorkian to catalyze change that leads to the appearance of more reasonable and likable physician reformers."

Massachusetts Vote May Change How the Nation Dies

Lewis M. Cohen

Lewis M. Cohen is an author, a Guggenheim fellow, and a professor at Tufts University. In the following viewpoint, he traces the history of the American right to die movement, beginning with the establishment of the Hemlock Society and moving to the radical actions of Jack Kevorkian, who was eventually jailed for helping terminally ill patients die. Cohen views Dr. Kevorkian as a revolutionary figure, who confronted the way the medical establishment treated death and dying. After Kevorkian, a new generation of physicians has come along, transformed by the death with dignity movement. These physicians have accepted that there is a role for physicians in this process, and that there is a time for some patients when palliative care is not the best option. When that time comes, Cohen contends that more physicians should have respect for patients' autonomy and self-determination and support them if they choose to end their own lives.

As you read, consider the following questions:

1. According to Cohen, what author kicked off the American right to die movement in the 1980s?

2. What does Cohen report was among Kate Morris's earliest lessons about suffering?

3. What percentage of Oregon patients who choose assisted dying die at home, according to the author?

This Election Day [November 2012], Massachusetts is poised to approve the death with dignity act. "Death with dignity" is a modernized, sanitized, politically palatable term that replaces the now-antiquated expression "physician-assisted suicide." Four polls conducted in the past couple of months have shown strong support for the ballot question, although a well-funded media blitz by the opposition is kicking in during the final several weeks and may influence voter opinions.

Oregon's Death with Dignity Act has been in effect for the past 14 years, and the state of Washington followed suit with a similar law in 2008. Despite concerns of skeptics, the sky has not fallen; civilization in the Northwest remains intact; the poor, disenfranchised, elderly, and vulnerable have not been victimized; and Oregon has become a leader in the provision of excellent palliative medicine services.

But the Massachusetts ballot question has the potential to turn death with dignity from a legislative experiment into the new national norm. The state is the home of America's leading medical publication (the *New England Journal of Medicine*), hospital (Massachusetts General), and four medical schools (Harvard, Boston University, University of Massachusetts, and

Tufts). Passage of the law would represent a crucial milestone for the death with dignity movement, especially since 42 percent of the state is Catholic and the church hierarchy vehemently opposes assisted dying. Vermont and New Jersey are already entertaining similar legislation, and if the act passes in Massachusetts, other states that have previously had unsuccessful campaigns will certainly be emboldened to revisit this subject. [Vermont passed a death with dignity law in 2013.]

The History of the Death with Dignity Movement

The American right to die movement began in the 1980s and 1990s with Derek Humphry's book, *Final Exit*, and his organization, the Hemlock Society. It was a reaction to a wave of technological advances, including antibiotics, antifungal medications, ventilators, dialysis machines, cardiopulmonary resuscitation, organ transplantation, and intensive care units. Death appeared to be on the run, cure was truly possible, and patients were politely requested to be quiet and allow physicians to heroically perform miracles. And that is when Dr. Jack Kevorkian—the bad boy of medicine—appeared on the scene.

Kevorkian was a revolutionary. He was beloved by patients and their families because of his gutsy intention to overthrow the medical establishment's prevailing ethos and hubris about dying. Clad in his nerdy, light-blue cardigan sweater, Kevorkian paraded in front of the cameras to show off homemade suicide gadgets and the Volkswagen van he occasionally drove on house calls to help suffering people end their lives. Before receiving an 11-to-20-year sentence for the second-degree murder of Thomas Youk, a 52-year-old Michigan accountant who suffered from amyotrophic lateral sclerosis (Lou Gehrig's disease), Judge Jessica Cooper said, "You had the audacity to go on national television, show the world what you did and dare the legal system to stop you. Well sir, consider yourself stopped."

So let's fast-forward to December 2007, when Cody Curtis was diagnosed with cholangiocarcinoma. This is an unusual and deadly cancer of the bile duct, the tube that runs through the liver. Depending on the size of the tumor and whether it has spread throughout the body, patients with this cancer are offered surgery, chemoradiation, and sometimes a liver transplant. Even with aggressive treatment, however, cholangiocarcinoma is usually a fatal diagnosis.

On a website called How We Die, Cody wrote with characteristic brio and wit:

> It's interesting how I was diagnosed—for my 52nd birthday I had gotten four, count them, four boxes of chocolate. And I ate them all. Afterwards I felt (deservedly) awful. I looked up my symptoms on the Internet and decided I was having a gall bladder attack like my father had earlier that year. It was a Saturday night so I didn't want to go to the emergency room.
>
> But I thought it was really weird, so a few weeks later I went in to see the doctor. She ordered an ultrasound. When I went back to her office to get the results, she looked at me and burst into tears. She said, "Your gall bladder's fine, but you have a big mass in your liver." The tumor was roughly the size of a grapefruit.

After Cody's primary care physician calmed down, she discussed the implications of the finding and referred her to a local oncology surgeon, Dr. Katherine Morris—whom Cody and her family came to know as Dr. Kate.

Cody's postings about her illness remained upbeat but realistic:

> The good news was the location of the tumor made a resection of my liver possible. Your liver regenerates and within six weeks you have a new liver. I had the first surgery, which cut out about 60 percent of my liver. But there were complications and I ended up in the hospital for 50 days. I couldn't

walk. I couldn't feed myself. My daughter lives in Washington D.C. She visited for a week and I didn't know she was there. And a year after the original surgery, the cancer came back, metastasized to the liver, lungs, and lymph nodes.

When Cody and Dr. Kate met for the first time, the surgeon was 39 years old. During the preceding three years, she had established a vibrant solo private practice based in Portland, Ore., while also helping run a research and tumor banking program at a tertiary care center. She was happily married and highly satisfied with her professional life.

Dr. Kate Morris

When I write medical stories, I routinely ask people to describe themselves and find that most physicians become flustered when asked this question. Although trained observers, doctors spend little time looking in a mirror or wryly considering their own appearance. They are no more or less narcissistic than the general public but rarely manage to put together a coherent description of themselves—let alone one that contains humor and modern cultural references. So I was delighted when Dr. Kate immediately responded: "I am hopeless at this, but will suggest, instead, a series of words to consider and words to avoid." Among the words and phrases to eschew were "stout, stumpy, Rubenesque, jolly, looks like Austin Powers minus the chest hair." Among those worthy of consideration are "a less anorexic Angelina Jolie, statuesque, willowy, serene, poised." She continued: "I'm 5'4" have dark, shoulder-length hair; kinda hazel eyes; and teeth I should have had straightened as a kid, but refused to have braces." This was followed by the admission that, "I've a tendency to be willful!"

Dr. Kate grew up in a bucolic setting on the outskirts of Olympia, Wash., in a home that abounded with horses, cats, and dogs. One of her earliest lessons was that you don't allow animals to suffer. She was raised as a Catholic and attended parochial school through eighth grade. She learned other lessons: People are responsible for themselves and their bodies, and autonomy is a cherished ethical principle to always be respected. Dr. Kate moved to Oregon to attend medical school and complete a surgical residency. She then traveled to New York City and Memorial Sloan Kettering [Cancer Center], where she did a surgical oncology fellowship focusing on cancers of the liver and pancreas. Portland, however, is not an easy city to leave, and she returned to establish a private practice and conduct clinical research. When Cody came to see Dr. Kate, she was one of a select group of surgeons specializing in the treatment of this particular kind of cancer.

A New Generation

Thanks to Cody's case, Dr. Kate is now among the pantheon of a growing number of medical professionals who have been transformed by death with dignity. Perhaps it takes the dramatic actions of a flawed advocate like Dr. Jack Kevorkian to catalyze change that leads to the appearance of more reasonable and likable physician reformers. Physicians of this new generation do not seek out or necessarily welcome the role, but, having accepted it, they are irreversibly changed. Most are modest, highly intellectual, and intensely private professionals who are drawn to medicine because it offers a challenge and an opportunity to help relieve distress. Most are workaholics who accept the drudgery and frequent frustrations of the profession because it is occasionally interrupted by the incomparable pleasure that comes with vanquishing an illness, ameliorating suffering, and saving a life. Few of these physicians would ever have dreamed that their greatest accomplishment might entail helping patients to die. Not one of them would have imagined him- or herself becoming a death with dignity advocate.

These doctors defy the deeply ingrained taboo against death and they are soft-spoken combatants in this professional

"Yes, I am a Doctor. Here's my card if you ever fancy dying."

© Grizelda/Cartoonstock.com.

and cultural war. The media has briefly illuminated a few of them. Dr. Timothy Quill is a bioethicist and primary care physician who wrote a provocative *New England Journal of Medicine* article that is death with dignity's literary equivalent of Harriet Beecher Stowe's *Uncle Tom's Cabin*. The first-person essay resulted in a grand jury investigation (he faced the possibility of indictment for murder or manslaughter), and it led to his eventual role as a plaintiff in a landmark U.S. Supreme Court case. Tim is this year's president of the American Academy of Hospice and Palliative Medicine.

Dr. Marcia Angell is another member of this group. She was the first female editor of the *New England Journal of Medicine* and has recently been attracting attention in her capacity as an eloquent spokesperson for the Massachusetts ballot question campaign. She fervently believes that it is vastly preferable for dying people to be offered a legal option of death with dignity than to secretly, fearfully, and often brutally kill themselves.

And then there is Dr. Kate Morris. At the time Cody became her patient, filmmaker Peter Richardson, a young native Oregonian, was absorbed by his state's decision to legalize death with dignity. Cody eagerly agreed to participate in his film, and Dr. Kate grudgingly acquiesced. Both women poignantly described to Peter the aftermath of the surgery, the complicated recuperation, the resumption of a vibrant life, and finally the recurrence of cancer. In the end, the camera respectfully hovered outside of Cody's bedroom, where her family gathered and where she ingested the lethal dose of barbiturates that allowed her the death with dignity she desired.

When I interviewed Richardson, he was still in shock that *How to Die in Oregon* had just received the Grand Jury Prize for documentary award at the 2011 Sundance Film Festival. Since then, it has been broadcast on HBO and is contending for an Emmy. At the festival, Dr. Kate shared a few intense minutes in the klieg lights with Cody Curtis' widower and her adult children, as they nervously answered audience questions.

Before moving to New Mexico for an academic position, the surgeon helped one more patient to use Oregon's Death with Dignity Act. She has since volunteered to be the lead physician plaintiff in a case challenging New Mexico's law against assisted dying.

The Role of Physicians in Dying

For people like Cody Curtis and Dr. Kate, death with dignity is not incompatible with palliative care, and data show that 90 percent of Oregon patients who choose assisted dying are simultaneously enrolled in hospice, and 95 percent die at home. Death with dignity epitomizes self-determination at a moment when palliative medicine bumps up against its limits, when patients are undergoing irremediable existential suffering and are in the process of losing everything that is meaningful to them.

After her patient's death, Dr. Kate concluded, "I think Cody taught me that 'first, do no harm,' is different for every patient. Harm for her would have meant taking away the control and saying, 'No, no, no! You have got to do this the way your body decides, as opposed to the way you as the person decides.'"

Dr. Kate's epiphany goes to the heart of the dilemma faced by physicians who are requested to assist in hastening dying. Most have been taught to adopt a passive stance and resist doing something rather than risk causing more harm than good. The ethical principle of non-maleficence has been a rationale for feigning deafness, and for ignoring or refusing to participate in a death with dignity [initiative]. However, Dr. Kate has realized that another, more important principle—respect for patient autonomy—should supersede in these cases. Whether or not you would consider assisted dying as a personal option, we should allow others to exercise their preferences. It is time we became pro-choice at the end of life.

> "Because so many doctors oppose as-
> sisted suicide, it's already tough to find
> doctors willing to assist in it—even
> where it's allowed."

Physicians Should Not Play a Role in Assisted Suicide

Chethan Sathya

Chethan Sathya is a surgical resident at the University of Toronto and a fellow in global journalism at the Munk School of Global Affairs. In the following viewpoint, he reports that doctors worldwide do not support the legalization of physician-assisted death, although in many countries the population overwhelmingly supports its legalization. Sathya attributes the high rate of opposition among physicians to major ethical concerns about killing patients and the overriding belief that a physician's role is to heal and protect, not to end life. He suggests that some physicians worry that legalizing physician-assisted death will lead to a slippery slope. Some people have proposed the idea of training non-doctors to assist in suicide administered by a central governing body, thus removing doctors from the equation completely, Sathya explains.

As you read, consider the following questions:

1. According to a survey by the Canadian Medical Association, what percentage of Canadian doctors would be willing to take part in assisted suicide?

2. According to a 2013 Environics Institute survey, what percentage of Canadians support physician-assisted suicide?

3. How many people does Sathya report were provided assisted-suicide services at Dignitas from 1998 to 2012?

As a doctor I can't help but wonder what I would do in a situation where physician-assisted suicide was legal. Given all my training to make patients healthier, could I assist in a patient's death with a clear conscience? To the contrary, if it helps a patient die with dignity, why wouldn't I help?

As the right to die debate picks up, recent surveys of doctors are raising an unsettling question: What happens if physician-assisted suicide becomes legal, even as most doctors remain deeply opposed to it?

Only 16 per cent of Canadian doctors would be willing to take part in assisted suicide, according to a March [2013] survey by the Canadian Medical Association. A *New England Journal of Medicine* survey in September found only 36 per cent of doctors in 74 countries were in favour of assisted suicide.

This places most doctors firmly out of step with public opinion. An Environics Institute survey in October showed that 69 per cent of Canadians support physician-assisted suicide, the highest recorded approval since 1992.

The gulf between popular support and doctors reminds some of how the abortion debate has played out in some regions where the procedure is legal but inaccessible. As with abortion, many doctors will refuse to participate, says Dr.

Donald Boudreau, an opponent of physician-assisted suicide who is a respirologist and the director of medical curriculum development at McGill University.

Assisted Suicide in Canada

Suicide is not illegal in Canada, but assisting in it is. Last year, the Supreme Court of British Columbia ruled against the ban on assisted suicide, saying it was unconstitutional. The B.C. Court of Appeal overturned the ruling in October. Quebec's right to die Bill 52 has added more fire to the debate. Before Toronto's well-known microbiologist Dr. Donald Low died from a brain tumor in September, he recorded a public plea for the right to die with dignity—prompting Ontario health minister Deb Matthews to suggest, "it's time to talk about assisted suicide."

Canada is joining a debate that has erupted across the world. Belgium, the Netherlands, Switzerland, Oregon, Washington State, Montana and, most recently, Vermont have all legalized physician-assisted suicide or euthanasia.

Many doctors who oppose assisted suicide have major ethical concerns about killing a patient, Boudreau says. The act is inherently against a physician's "do no harm" principle, he adds. "How can I teach medical students about healing when I have to prepare them as euthanizers?" he asks.

Vulnerable Populations?

People become doctors to support human beings in their darkest hour, says Dr. Margaret Cottle, a palliative care doctor from Vancouver and vice president of the Euthanasia Prevention Coalition. "There is something so deeply human about that connection, and to take it away with a lethal pill, instead of supporting patients through these difficult periods, will destroy us," she adds.

Some doctors also worry that assisted-suicide laws could be misused. In the Netherlands and Belgium, euthanasia is be-

Suicide Tourism

The Swiss government has announced that it will take steps to oversee the growing trend of what it calls "suicide tourism" in its country. Hundreds of people from across Europe—more than one hundred from the United Kingdom alone—have visited the Swiss facility Dignitas in order to take advantage of its assisted-suicide services. The minister of justice has called for stricter controls on organizations like Dignitas to make it harder for potential customers to qualify for assisted suicide. The justice minister said that new laws would restrict but not ban assisted suicide in Switzerland.

"Assisted Suicide and Euthanasia,"
Global Issues in Context Online Collection, 2014.

ing administered to patients with mental illness who do not necessarily have a terminal illness, Cottle says. She highlights the recently publicized case of Nathan Verhelst, a 44-year-old who was legally euthanized in Belgium after a botched sex-change operation resulted in "unbearable psychological suffering," according to reports in the media.

Opponents also worry that vulnerable populations, such as the elderly and poor, may be pressured into a duty to die as opposed to a right to die. "Having been at the bedside of dying patients for 25 years, I can tell you that these patients are extremely vulnerable and depressed," Cottle says. Opening up the possibility of assisted suicide will pressure patients to choose to live or die—in many cases as a result of financial or emotional burden on their families, she fears.

Doctors who support the decriminalization of assisted suicide, such as Dr. James Downar, a palliative and critical care doctor at Toronto General Hospital, have a different view.

Doctors can often treat stable symptoms such as pain, but some patients develop sudden complications, and "we cannot always ensure that they will die without symptoms," Downar says. He adds that most people who request assisted suicide are concerned about the loss of independence and control, something that can't be treated.

Downar does not believe that misuse will occur with carefully thought-out laws. "There is always a potential for abuse of the law, but data from Oregon and Washington don't support this. It remains an option taken by less than one per cent of the population, most of whom are educated, white men," he says.

Cottle disagrees. Even in Oregon and Washington, the laws allow for abuses to occur, she says. There is no oversight of the lethal medications—once patients pick up their drugs, they take them home and can use them whenever they please, she says. When a patient dies, there is no recall of the lethal drugs by the pharmacy, making it uncertain what killed the patient and where the drugs ended up, she says. There will be abuses, it's just not reported, she adds.

If assisted suicide is legalized, disagreeing doctors could be pushed into a corner. While laws allowing physician-assisted suicide also let individual doctors refuse to participate, most require doctors to refer patients to others who will perform it.

This obligation to refer could force doctors into an ethical quandary, Boudreau says. And doctors may be hesitant to work in hospitals that offer assisted suicide. "Ask yourself, how would I feel if I were all of a sudden working in a hospital that . . . started to do something that I found morally reprehensible?" Boudreau asks.

Because so many doctors oppose assisted suicide, it's already tough to find doctors willing to assist in it—even where it's allowed.

In March 2012, the Netherlands euthanasia lobby NVVE set up mobile clinics to provide assisted suicide to patients who had been refused by their doctors. Compassion & Choices, a U.S. nonprofit organization, has launched campaigns in Montana, Washington State and Oregon using poignant pleas from patients to pressure doctors into assisting suicide.

Switzerland may have found a way to avoid unwilling doctors and hospitals altogether. Organizations such as Dignitas, founded by Swiss lawyer Ludwig A. Minelli, recruit volunteers to help people commit suicide. Willing doctors still have to prescribe the lethal drugs but don't participate directly. Dignitas performs the procedure in private clinics outside hospitals. From 1998 to 2012, it provided assisted suicide to 1,496 people.

Some observers propose removing doctors completely from the equation. Alternative methods, such as using non-doctors to assist in suicide through a centralized government body, need to be considered, Boudreau says. "Why do doctors need to be the ones performing this?" he asks.

Dr. Lisa Lehmann, director of the Center for Bioethics at Brigham and Women's Hospital in Boston, touted this idea in the July 2012 *New England Journal of Medicine*. She suggested that physicians could certify a patient's diagnosis and prognosis, and patients could then use an independent authority to get a prescription for suicide drugs.

When Cottle is asked by patients to assist in their suicide, she tells them that today they may not feel like living, but who knows how they will feel one month from now. "What if a grandchild is born, or a graduation happens, or someone close to you gets married, wouldn't you want to be there?" she asks.

Determining prognosis is never easy, so providing patients with a definite timeline to death is near impossible, Cottle says. "The end-of-life experience is like being on a tightrope with no net, if there is no wind, you can stay on that rope for quite a long time," she says.

Periodical and Internet Sources Bibliography

The following articles have been selected to supplement the diverse views presented in this chapter.

Heather Beasley Doyle   "Right to Die: Netherlands, Belgium Ignite Global Debate on Euthanasia," *Al Jazeera America*, March 4, 2014.

Erik Eckholm   "New Mexico Judge Affirms Right to 'Aid in Dying,'" *New York Times*, January 13, 2014.

Michael Gonchar   "Should Physician-Assisted Suicide Be Legal in Every State?," *New York Times*, October 24, 2014.

Barbara Kay   "Euthanasia's Damage to the Human Soul," *National Post* (Toronto), September 30, 2014.

Eugene Kontorovich   "What Belgium's Child Euthanasia Law Means for America and the Constitution," *Washington Post*, February 13, 2014.

Scott Martelle   "Extend Assisted Suicide to Children? Belgium Says Yes; So Should We," *Los Angeles Times*, February 14, 2014.

Art Moore   "Expert: Child Euthanasia a 'Logical Progression,'" WND.com, February 13, 2014.

Steven Reinberg   "Most Doctors Oppose Physician-Assisted Suicide, Poll Finds," HealthDay, September 11, 2013.

Tom Riddington   "Euthanasia for Children Is Hard to Contemplate—but We Must Talk About It," *Guardian* (UK), February 17, 2014.

Wesley J. Smith   "Some Dutch Pharmacists Say No to Euthanasia," *National Review Online*, April 16, 2014.

OPPOSING
VIEWPOINTS®
SERIES

CHAPTER 4

How Does the Affordable Care Act Affect the Euthanasia Debate?

Chapter Preface

On July 16, 2009, Betsy McCaughey, the former lieutenant governor of New York, went on a conservative radio show to talk about the Patient Protection and Affordable Care Act, commonly known as the Affordable Care Act (ACA) or Obamacare. During the discussion, she implied that the ACA would be terrible for older Americans because it would cut off health insurance coverage for the elderly. It was, she accused, a "vicious attack on elderly people." A week later, she reiterated her charge in the *New York Post*. In an op-ed, she predicted that the bill would result in health care rationing, a system in which the healthy and young would receive the best medical care and the disabled and elderly would be discriminated against out of distorted ideas of social justice. She went on to say that in effect, a government panel of bureaucrats would be making life-and-death decisions that could impact American families—a troubling charge that would later explode into what is known as the death panel controversy.

The ACA is a landmark reform of the health care system of the United States. The legislation aims to expand private and public health insurance coverage, cut health care costs, and increase the affordability of health insurance for businesses, families, and individuals through subsidies and exchanges that lower insurance premiums for most Americans. Critics of the ACA predicted that the new system would fail to control costs and would result in cancelled health insurance policies, skyrocketing premiums, and the rationing of health care services.

The ACA provoked a heated debate that largely broke down in a partisan manner: Republicans overwhelmingly opposed the bill, and Democrats favored it. The debate dominated political coverage in 2009, spurring charges and countercharges on political talk radio, television, and other media.

McCaughey's accusation that the ACA would limit health care for the elderly and disabled can be traced to provisions in early drafts of the bill that proposed a board to review the effectiveness and costs of certain medical treatments and a plan to reimburse Medicare for providing counseling on end-of-life issues, such as living wills and advance directives. These two provisions were conflated and reinterpreted by McCaughey and then amplified by Representative Michele Bachmann on the floor of the US House of Representatives a few days later. McCaughey's accusations that the health care rationing would endanger the sick, elderly, and disabled were repeated by several conservative lawmakers in the following days.

On August 7, 2009, the issue erupted into widespread controversy when former Alaskan governor and vice-presidential candidate Sarah Palin wrote a Facebook post repeating the accusation that the ACA would set up a government panel to ration health care, which would likely result in many people, especially the elderly and disabled, being refused lifesaving care.

"Government health care will not reduce the cost; it will simply refuse to pay the cost," Palin wrote. "And who will suffer the most when they ration care? The sick, the elderly, and the disabled, of course. The America I know and love is not one in which my parents or my baby with Down syndrome will have to stand in front of Obama's 'death panel' so his bureaucrats will decide, based on a subjective judgment of their 'level of productivity in society,' whether they are worthy of health care. Such a system is downright evil."

Palin's accusations of death panels in the ACA were immediately refuted by supporters of the law, who pointed out that none of the provisions in the bill provided for a system to determine if patients were "worthy of health care." A number of media sources also derided Palin's use of the term, calling it misleading and inflammatory. The prominent fact-checking site PolitiFact.com deemed it to be "The Lie of the Year" for

2009 and said of Palin's remarks, "Her assertion—that the government would set up boards to determine whether seniors and the disabled were worthy of care—spread through newscasts, talk shows, blogs, and town hall meetings. Opponents of healthcare legislation said it revealed the real goals of the Democratic proposals. Advocates for health reform said that it showed the depths to which their opponents would sink. Still others scratched their heads and said, 'Death panels? Really?'"

The debate over whether the ACA would create death panels that would ration health care for the sick, elderly, and the disabled is one of the topics explored in the following chapter, which scrutinizes the impact of the ACA on the issue of euthanasia. Other viewpoints in the chapter examine the value of end-of-life planning and the ACA's overall influence on the death with dignity movement.

> *"In the United States, keeping an all-but-dead patient alive on life support in a hospital bed generates income for the hospital."*

Canada Has Death Panels

Adam Goldenberg

Adam Goldenberg is a former political speechwriter and law student. In the following viewpoint, he notes that while some Americans have been up in arms over the charge that the Patient Protection and Affordable Care Act creates death panels, Canada has had such panels for years without major controversy. In the Canadian province of Ontario, the legislature put in place the Consent and Capacity Board, a panel made up of lawyers, mental health professionals, and community members that adjudicates disputes on end-of-life decisions. A recent court decision further defined the role of the Consent and Capacity Board, ruling that it has the right to overrule the decision of the primary decision maker, usually a spouse or close family member. Goldenberg argues that such panels are a practical and efficient solution for a complex and often heart-wrenching problem.

As you read, consider the following questions:

1. According to the author, what former Republican vice-presidential candidate made the term "death panels" famous in the United States?

2. In what year did Ontario create the Consent and Capacity Board?

3. How did the Supreme Court of Canada rule on the fate of Hassan Rasouli?

L ast week [in October 2013] Canada's Supreme Court ruled that doctors could not unilaterally ignore a Toronto family's decision to keep their near-dead husband and father on life support. In the same breath, however, the court also confirmed that, under the laws of Ontario, Canada's most populous province, a group of government-appointed adjudicators could yet overrule the family's choice. That tribunal, not the family or the doctors, has the ultimate power to pull the plug.

In other words: Canada has death panels.

Death Panels: The Canadian Version

I use that term advisedly. Former Republican vice-presidential candidate Sarah Palin made it famous in the summer of 2009, when Congress was fighting over whether to pass Obamacare [referring to the Patient Protection and Affordable Care Act, commonly known as the Affordable Care Act]. As Republicans and Democrats continue to spar over health care, we should pause to wonder why millions of Canadians have come to accept the functional equivalent of an idea that almost sank health care reform even though, in this country, it was imaginary.

Ontario's Health Care Consent Act has been on the books for nearly two decades. Like similar laws in many Canadian provinces—and American states—it sets out the process for making treatment decisions when a patient cannot provide or withhold her consent—when she is in a coma and on life support, for example. In such cases, power automatically shifts to a "substitute decision maker," usually a close relative. When these family members disagree with a patient's doctors, and when the doctors are nonetheless determined to act, the dispute generally goes to court, where it can take months or even years to resolve. That is how it works in other Canadian and American jurisdictions, anyway. In Ontario, by contrast, the provincial legislature decided in 1996 to create a quasi-judicial tribunal, the Consent and Capacity Board, to make these life-and-death decisions more quickly. If a patient's substitute decision maker withholds consent, then doctors may apply to the board—comprised of lawyers, mental health professionals, and community members—for a determination that the proposed treatment is in the patient's best interest. If so, the board has the power to consent on the patient's behalf.

At issue in the Ontario case was the fate of Hassan Rasouli, a retired engineer who has been comatose in a Toronto hospital since he suffered complications following brain surgery three years ago. When Rasouli's doctors determined that he had no reasonable prospect of recovery, they sought to pull the plug. His family, convinced that Rasouli was slowly recovering, took his doctors to court.

The Court Ruling

Last Friday, they won. The Supreme Court of Canada ruled 5–2 that Ontario doctors may not decide to withhold treatment from patients in Rasouli's condition without consent from the next-in-line decision maker. In Rasouli's case, that is his wife. But, if she refuses consent, then her husband's doctors can still ask for a ruling from Ontario's Consent and Capacity Board. The Supreme Court confirmed last week that the board has the power to overrule her.

National Health Care Systems

Many industrialized nations have national health insurance systems. Most national health care plans guarantee minimal national health insurance to all citizens, though some provide insurance only to people with low incomes. Many countries that provide national health insurance allow citizens to purchase supplemental private insurance. Countries that have national health insurance plans include Australia, Japan, China, Cuba, Sweden, Russia, the United Kingdom, Germany, the Netherlands, Austria, Sri Lanka, Chile, Thailand, and Canada. Canada's system is acclaimed for its effectiveness in affording health care access to all and has been successful in keeping the population healthy, though critics say the quality of health care under a national health care program is diminished. Cuba, a developing nation, adopted a national health care system in the mid-1970s with the revised Cuban constitution, which guarantees everyone the right to health care. The country's population enjoys greater health than many nations of similar or higher economic status.

"Access to Health Care,"
Global Issues in Context Online Collection, 2014.

Most media coverage of the Canadian ruling has focused on the first part—that doctors cannot overrule family members—rather than the second—that an administrative tribunal can. Most Ontarians are evidently content with—or indifferent to, or simply ignorant of—the fact that the Consent and Capacity Board has the power to make difficult, even existential, health care decisions on behalf of patients who are still (technically) alive. Americans, I expect, would be apoplectic.

In Canada, with our single-payer health care system, Rasouli's situation has a very public bottom line: Should taxpayers foot the bill for his family's indefinite goodbye?

But American critics of Canadian health care will declare that merely asking this question is unacceptable, unethical, even unthinkable—and that it proves that the Canadian system gives doctors a dangerous incentive to kill off their patients as quickly as possible. They are wrong. The Hippocratic Oath's promise to do no harm still applies. But they are also only wrong in part. When taxpayers provide only a finite number of acute care beds in public hospitals, a patient whose life has all but ended, but whose family insists on keeping her on life support, is occupying precious space that might otherwise house a patient whose best years are still ahead.

The incentives in the American health care system point in the opposite direction. In the United States, keeping an all-but-dead patient alive on life support in a hospital bed generates income for the hospital, for as long as its bills get paid.

Ontario's Consent and Capacity Board provides an objective process for resolving these difficult, end-of-life dilemmas. The board is instructed by law to focus on the patient's best interests, not the health care system's, nor the government's bottom line. Still, the law recognizes that, though it is usually in the patient's best interests to be kept alive, it is not always so. As Rasouli's doctors told the Supreme Court, prolonging his life would entail the risk of infection, bedsores, and organ failure. When recovery is out of the question, in other words, there may be fates worse than death.

A Better System for Canadians

Yet, the question remains: Who decides? Remember that, outside of Ontario, the resolution of these end-of-life disputes is generally reserved for judges. Ontario has simply replaced them with experts and wise community members. That's a lead other jurisdictions should consider following when families' emotions and doctors' judgments collide.

Perhaps it is easier for Canadians to trust government-appointed panels, rather than judges, with decisions like these. For reasons that arguably go back to our respective foundings, Canadians tend to have more faith in our government and our bureaucratic processes than Americans do in theirs. Look at gun control: Canada lacks a constitutional guarantee of a right to bear arms in part because we never fought a war of independence that made one seem necessary. Similarly, when conservative politicians in the United States condemn Obamacare as a "government takeover" of health care, a lot of Canadians roll our eyes.

Still, the Rasouli family's situation is familiar, and it will only become more commonplace. Modern medicine increasingly allows us to extend life indefinitely, and so the question is no longer whether we can "play God," but when, how, and who should do so. When humanity demands haste, and justice demands expert knowledge, Ontario's death panels offer a solution—whatever Sarah Palin says.

| "As long as health care is viewed as a product to be bought and sold, even the most well-intentioned reformers will someday soon have to come to grips with health care rationing."

Death Panels Are Inevitable as Long as Health Care Is Considered a Commodity

James Ridgeway

James Ridgeway is an author, award-winning journalist, and a former senior correspondent for Mother Jones. *In the following viewpoint, he suggests that as long as the United States treats health care as a commodity there will be health care rationing. This doesn't exist in most other industrialized countries because they view health care as a human right and share the costs and benefits among all citizens. In the United States, however, health care is a commodity, and it is the wealthy who get all the benefits because they can afford top treatments and services. Meanwhile, the rest of Americans are often pitted against each other to procure adequate treatment—and the elderly are often at the losing end of this battle because chronic illness and end-of-life treatments are very expensive.*

As you read, consider the following questions:

1. According to Ridgeway, what percentage of each GDP dollar does the United States spend on health care?

2. How much of annual Medicare expenditures does the author report is spent on patients with fewer than thirty days to live?

3. According to the Dartmouth Atlas of Health Care, how much less medical expenditures do patients in Oregon run up than those in other states?

There's a certain age at which you cease to regard your own death as a distant hypothetical and start to view it as a coming event. For me, it was 67—the age at which my father died. For many Americans, I suspect it's 70—the age that puts you within striking distance of our average national life expectancy of 78.1 years. Even if you still feel pretty spry, you suddenly find that your roster of doctors' appointments has expanded, along with your collection of daily medications. You grow accustomed to hearing that yet another person you once knew has dropped off the twig. And you feel more and more like a walking ghost yourself, invisible to the younger people who push past you on the subway escalator. Like it or not, death becomes something you think about, often on a daily basis.

Actually, you don't think about death, per se, as much as you do about dying—about when and where and especially *how* you're going to die. Will you have to deal with a long illness? With pain, immobility, or dementia? Will you be able to get the care you need, and will you have enough money to pay for it? Most of all, will you lose control over what life you have left, as well as over the circumstances of your death?

These are precisely the preoccupations that the right so cynically exploited in the debate over health care reform, with that ominous talk of Washington bean counters deciding who lives and dies. It was all nonsense, of course—the worst kind of political scare tactic. But at the same time, supporters of health care reform seemed to me too quick to dismiss old people's fears as just so much paranoid foolishness. There are reasons why the death panel myth found fertile ground—and those reasons go beyond the gullibility of half-senile old farts.

Health Care as a Commodity

While politicians of all stripes shun the idea of health care rationing as the political third rail that it is, most of them accept a premise that leads, one way or another, to that end. Here's what I mean: Nearly every other industrialized country recognizes health care as a human right, whose costs and benefits are shared among all citizens. But in the United States, the leaders of both political parties along with most of the "experts" persist in treating health care as a commodity that is purchased, in one way or another, by those who can afford it. Conservatives embrace this notion as the perfect expression of the all-powerful market; though they make a great show of recoiling from the term, in practice they are endorsing rationing on the basis of wealth. Liberals, including supporters of President [Barack] Obama's health care reform, advocate subsidies, regulation, and other modest measures to give the less fortunate a little more buying power. But as long as health care is viewed as a product to be bought and sold, even the most well-intentioned reformers will someday soon have to come to grips with health care rationing, if not by wealth then by some other criteria.

In a country that already spends more than 16 percent of each GDP [gross domestic product] dollar on health care, it's easy to see why so many people believe there's simply not enough of it to go around. But keep in mind that the rest of the industrialized world manages to spend between 20 and 90 percent less per capita and still rank higher than the US in overall health care performance. In 2004, a team of researchers including Princeton's Uwe Reinhardt, one of the nation's best-known experts on health economics, found that while the US spends 134 percent more than the median of the world's most developed nations, we get less for our money—fewer physician visits and hospital days per capita, for example—than our counterparts in countries like Germany, Canada, and Australia. (We do, however, have more MRI machines and more cesarean sections.)

Where Does the Money Go?

Where does the money go instead? By some estimates, administration and insurance profits alone eat up at least 30 percent of our total health care bill (and most of that is in the private sector—Medicare's overhead is around 2 percent). In other words, we don't have too little to go around—we overpay for what we get, and we don't allocate our spending where it does us the most good. "In most [medical] resources we have a surplus," says Dr. David Himmelstein, cofounder of Physicians for a National Health Program. "People get large amounts of care that don't do them any good and might cause them harm [while] others don't get the necessary amount."

Looking at the numbers, it's pretty safe to say that with an efficient health care system, we could spend a little less than we do now and provide all Americans with the most spectacular care the world has ever known. But in the absence of any serious challenge to the health-care-as-commodity system, we are doomed to a battlefield scenario where Americans must fight to secure their share of a "scarce" resource in a life-and-death struggle that pits the rich against the poor, the insured against the uninsured—and increasingly, the old against the young.

Making Untenable Connections

For years, any push to improve the nation's finances—balance the budget, pay for the bailout, or help stimulate the economy—has been accompanied by rumblings about the greedy geezers who resist entitlement "reforms" (read: cuts) with their unconscionable demands for basic health care and a hedge against destitution. So, too, today: Already, President Obama's newly convened deficit commission looks to be blaming the nation's fiscal woes not on tax cuts, wars, or bank bailouts, but on the burden of Social Security and Medicare. (The commission's cochair, former Republican senator Alan Simpson, has declared, "This country is gonna go to the bow-wows unless we deal with entitlements.")

Old people's anxiety in the face of such hostile attitudes has provided fertile ground for Republican disinformation and fearmongering. But so has the vacuum left by Democratic reformers. Too often, in their zeal to prove themselves tough on "waste," they've allowed connections to be drawn between two things that, to my mind, should never be spoken of in the same breath: *death* and *cost*.

Dying Wishes

The death panel myth started with a harmless minor provision in the health reform bill that required Medicare to pay in case enrollees wanted to have conversations with their own doctors about "advance directives" like health care proxies and living wills. The controversy that ensued, thanks to a host of right-wing commentators and Sarah Palin's Facebook page, ensured that the advance-planning measure was expunged from the bill. But the underlying debate didn't end with the passage of health care reform, any more than it began there. For if rationing is inevitable once you've ruled out reining in private profits, the question is, who should be denied care, and at what point? And given that no one will publicly argue for withholding cancer treatment from a seven-year-old, the answer almost inevitably seems to come down to what we spend on people—*old* people—in their final years.

As far back as 1983, in a speech to the Health Insurance Association of America, a then 57-year-old Alan Greenspan suggested that we consider "whether it is worth it" to spend so much of Medicare's outlays on people who would die within the year. (Appropriately, Ayn Rand called her acolyte "the undertaker"—though she chose the nickname because of his dark suits and austere demeanor.)

Not everyone puts the issue in such nakedly pecuniary terms, but in an April 2009 interview with the *New York Times Magazine*, Obama made a similar point in speaking of end-of-life care as a "huge driver of cost." He said, "The chronically ill and those toward the end of their lives are accounting for potentially 80 percent of the total health care bill out here."

The Economic Reality of Dying

The president was being a bit imprecise: Those figures are actually for Medicare expenditures, not the total health care tab, and more important, lumping the dying together with the "chronically ill"—who often will live for years or decades—makes little sense. But there is no denying that end-of-life care is expensive. Hard numbers are not easy to come by, but studies from the 1990s suggest that between a quarter and a third of annual Medicare expenditures go to patients in their last year of life, and 30 to 40 percent of *those* costs accrue in the final month. What this means is that around one in ten Medicare dollars—some $50 billion a year—are spent on patients with fewer than 30 days to live.

Pronouncements on these data usually come coated with a veneer of compassion and concern: How *terrible* it is that all those poor dying old folks have to endure aggressive treatments that only delay the inevitable; all we want to do is bring peace and dignity to their final days! But I wonder: If that's really what they're worried about, how come they keep talking about money?

The Right to Die

At this point, I ought to make something clear: I am a big fan of what's sometimes called the "right to die" or "death with

"Bloody humans! Taking our jobs!"

© Grizelda/Cartoonstock.com.

dignity" movement. I support everything from advance directives to assisted suicide. You could say I believe in one form of health care rationing: the kind you choose for yourself. I can't stand the idea of anyone—whether it's the government or some hospital administrator or doctor or Nurse Jackie [a television character] telling me that I must have some treatment I don't want, any more than I want them telling me that I can't have a treatment I *do* want. My final wish is to be my own one-member death panel.

A physician friend recently told me about a relative of hers, a frail 90-year-old woman suffering from cancer. Her doctors urged her to have surgery, followed by treatment with a recently approved cancer medicine that cost $5,000 a month. As is often the case, my friend said, the doctors told their patient about the benefits of the treatment, but not about all the risks—that she might die during the surgery or not long afterward. They also prescribed a month's supply of the new medication, even though, my friend says, they must have known the woman was unlikely to live that long. She died within a week. "Now," my friend said, "I'm carrying around a $4,000 bottle of pills."

Perhaps reflecting what economists call "supplier-induced demand," costs generally tend to go up when the dying have too *little* control over their care, rather than too much. When geezers are empowered to make decisions, most of us will choose less aggressive—and less costly—treatments. If we don't do so more often, it's usually because of an overbearing and money-hungry health care system, as well as a culture that disrespects the will of its elders and resists confronting death.

The Principle of Self-Determination

Once, when I was in the hospital for outpatient surgery, I woke up in the recovery area next to a man named George, who was talking loudly to his wife, telling her he wanted to leave. She soothingly reminded him that they had to wait for the doctors to learn the results of the surgery, apparently some sort of exploratory thing. Just then, two doctors appeared. In a stiff, flat voice, one of them told George that he had six months to live. When his wife's shrieking had subsided, I heard George say, "I'm getting the f--- out of this place." The doctors sternly advised him that they had more tests to run and "treatment options" to discuss. "F--- that," said George, yanking the IV out of his arm and getting to his feet. "If I've got six months to live, do you think I want to spend another minute of it here? I'm going to the Alps to go skiing."

I don't know whether George was true to his word. But not long ago I had a friend, a scientist, who was true to his. Suffering from cancer, he anticipated a time when more chemotherapy or procedures could only prolong a deepening misery, to the point where he could no longer recognize himself. He prepared for that time, hoarding his pain meds, taking care to protect his doctor and pharmacist from any possibility of legal retribution. He saw some friends he wanted to see, and spoke to others. Then he died at a time and place of his choosing, with his family around him. Some would call this euthanasia, others a sacrilege. To me, it seemed like a noble end to a fine life. If freedom of choice is what makes us human, then my friend managed to make his death a final expression of his humanity.

My friend chose to forgo medical treatments that would have added many thousands of dollars to his health care costs—and, since he was on Medicare, to the public expense. If George really did spend his final months in the Alps, instead of undergoing expensive surgeries or sitting around hooked up to machines, he surely saved the health care system a bundle as well. They did it because it was what they wanted, not because it would save money. But there is a growing body of evidence that the former can lead to the latter—without any rationing or coercion.

A New Model

One model that gets cited a lot these days is La Crosse, Wisconsin, where Gundersen Lutheran hospital launched an initiative to ensure that the town's older residents had advance directives and to make hospice and palliative care widely available. A 2008 study found that 90 percent of those who died in La Crosse under a physician's care did so with advance directives in place. At Gundersen Lutheran, less is spent on patients in their last two years of life than nearly any other place in the US, with per capita Medicare costs 30 percent below the national average. In a similar vein, Oregon in 1995 instituted a two-page form called "Physician Orders for Life-Sustaining Treatment"; it functions as doctor's orders and is less likely to be misinterpreted or disregarded than a living will. According to the Dartmouth Atlas of Health Care, a 20-year study of the nation's medical costs and resources, people in Oregon are less likely to die in a hospital than people in most other states, and in their last six months, they spend less time in the hospital. They also run up about 50 percent less in medical expenditures.

It's possible that attitudes have begun to change. . . . More Americans than ever have living wills and other advance directives, and that can only be a good thing: One recent study showed that more than 70 percent of patients who needed to make end-of-life decisions at some point lost the capacity to make these choices, yet among those who had prepared living wills, nearly all had their instructions carried out.

Here is the ultimate irony of the death panel meme: In attacking measures designed to promote advance directives, conservatives were attacking what they claim is their core value—the individual right to free choice.

> "The bill had no death panels. There
> was simply a plan to consult a doctor
> every five years for end-of-life plan-
> ning."

The Affordable Care Act
Death Panels Are a Myth

Linda Milazzo

Linda Milazzo is an educator and journalist. In the following viewpoint, she states that the Patient Protection and Affordable Care Act, commonly known as the Affordable Care Act (ACA) or Obamacare, does not have death panels, only a plan to consult a doctor every five years for end-of-life planning. Milazzo maintains that this proposed counseling, which was meant to bring information and comfort to patients and their families, was attacked by conservative critics and twisted into the concept of "death panels," a lie that was meant to scare Americans and turn people against the health care bill. She claims the media was complicit in this effort by amplifying the views of partisan politicians and commentators willing to lie about the ACA and by failing to correct the misinformation. Milazzo relates a story of her mother's painful and prolonged death, suggesting that the issues of death and dying and accessibility to health care are too important to allow campaigns of misinformation to influence public opinion.

As you read, consider the following questions:

1. According to Milazzo, to what female politician did the media provide air time to amplify her false claims of "death panels" being part of the Affordable Care Act?

2. What did the Medicare regulation that President Obama issued on January 1, 2012, direct?

3. What disease did Milazzo's mother die from in 1977?

Across America, people suffer end-of-life illness. They agonize in pain. They agonize in fear. They're in drug induced stupors. Modest people soil themselves in front of friends and family. They avert their eyes in shame. They lose and regain consciousness. They welcome the unconscious moments that shield them from feelings of helplessness and burdening those they love.

This is no way to live. This is no way to die.

Throughout the recent debate on the health care bill [the Patient Protection and Affordable Care Act], the media—in particular cable TV and talk radio—inflamed the rhetoric on the bill; on the bill's size, its number of pages, its fiscal impact, its social impact, excluding abortion, surviving death panels. . . .

Death panels?!

The bill had no death panels. There was simply a plan to consult a doctor every five years for end-of-life planning. That was it. Sensitive, helpful, humane, necessary, professional end-of-life planning to comfort and protect the dying and guide their families through a difficult time.

The Influence of Media on the Health Care Debate

But corporate media perverted the plan. It afforded Sarah Palin, media's most caustic creation, round-the-clock amplification of her death panel misnomer. Rather than quell Palin's toxic distortions and present the plan factually by name and content, corporate media appropriated Palin's death panel fabrication and amplified it even more, spending weeks misrepresenting the plan and rendering it unrecognizable from its original form.

Eventually, corporate media's constant drumming of death panel lies resulted in Section 1233 (which allowed Medicare to provide advance planning doctor visits every five years) being eliminated from the Patient Protection and Affordable Care Act that passed in 2010.

On Christmas Day, the *New York Times* reported that President [Barack] Obama would issue a Medicare regulation January 1st, which provides that "the government will pay doctors who advise patients on options for end-of-life care, which may include advance directives to forgo aggressive life-sustaining treatment." Sadly, but not surprisingly, corporate media didn't hesitate to jump on this report and revive the death panel deception. . . .

Enough, CNN! Enough! Stop trivializing and dramatizing critical issues. . . . Report the news. Report the truth and stop whoring your twisted wares in the name of journalism. This isn't journalism.

This is media destruction, fact distortion and public denigration. Americans don't need this. Our nation's sliding into ruins and you ruin it even more.

This is my *Network* moment. *I'm mad as hell and I'm not going to take it anymore* from CNN, MSNBC, Fox, NBC, ABC, CBS and talk radio. We the people deserve better.

Sarah Palin

No one rose or fell faster in American politics than Sarah Palin. Elected governor of Alaska in 2006, the young reform-minded politician quickly become widely admired by conservative political thinkers. When Republican presidential candidate John McCain needed to shake up the campaign in August of 2008, he rejected several more experienced politicians and asked Palin to become his running mate. After a dramatic debut at the Republican National Convention, Palin suddenly became a polarizing national figure. Conservatives saw her as an exciting agent of change and liberals considered her unqualified for the position she sought. After McCain and Palin lost the 2008 election, Palin found the politics of Alaska and the pressures of fame difficult. In June of 2009, she shocked America by resigning, saying a rash of ethics complaints against her and other criticism had become too distracting for her to do her job. She continued to focus on politics, which sparked rumors of a bid for the presidency. Palin formed SarahPAC, a political action committee.

"Sarah Palin,"
Gale Biography in Context Online, 2014.

This wretched corporate media cheered us into Iraq. It's made downtown Manhattan the flash point for xenophobia and racism over the building of a community center intended to unify neighbors. It's given a platform to birthers. It's undermined global warming. It's created the monster Sarah Palin and it craves creating more. It's desecrating the living and it's desecrating the dying.

Enough!

A Personal Story

My mother died in 1977. She had cancer. Before she died, I flew to her hospital bed in New York. When I arrived at the hospital, I ran down the hall and charged into her room. I hadn't seen her in months. She was surrounded by family. My knees buckled the instant I saw her. A relative caught me and carried me into the hall. I shook from head to toe. My mother was a skeleton.

We took her home from the hospital. Her sister flew in to help care for her. The last months of her life were living hell. She was robbed of her dignity. She was ashamed of being helpless, of needing to be fed and bathed, of being seen naked. She couldn't look us in the eye.

After a while, the weak pain killers the doctor prescribed couldn't stop her pain. I drove to her doctor's office in the snow and demanded a stronger medication. He prescribed injectable morphine. I took the prescription and had it filled. Later that day, a visiting nurse came to teach me to inject my mother. We rehearsed on the skin of an orange. That night my mother cried in pain. I went to her with the syringe and told her to relax; that it would be okay. She was semiconscious.

I filled the syringe and positioned myself to inject her. I was shaking. My tears clouded my eyes. I held the syringe to her skin and *I missed*. At that moment my mother came to. She looked at me and said, "it's okay." I was never able to inject her. Her suffering went on. . . .

My family's story is not unique. This happens every day to families across our nation. Millions have similar stories, and yet our media, our whoring media, for ad revenue and ratings, trivialize and falsify the truth. About death. About war. About our planet. About what Americans want.

It's time to stop this madness!

| "*Unfortunately, health care rationing is going to contribute to the increasing number of premature deaths in health care settings.*"

ObamaCare Is to Euthanasia What *Roe v. Wade* Was to Abortion

Brian J. Kopp

Brian J. Kopp is a podiatrist as well as a political and social commentator. In the following viewpoint, he urges activists in the pro-life movement to turn their attention to the issue of stealth euthanasia. Kopp argues that with the implementation of the Patient Protection and Affordable Care Act, commonly known as the Affordable Care Act (ACA) or Obamacare, health care will be inevitably rationed. He fears that Americans in hospice care will be the ones that will be the victims of health care rationing, evinced by the higher percentage of patients dying in hospice care every year. This trend, he believes, is evidence of stealth euthanasia—overmedication, terminal sedation, and withdrawal of hydration and nutrition—being practiced by medical professionals in palliative care settings. Under the ACA, he predicts that stealth euthanasia will be the norm unless the pro-life movement mobilizes and works to change the growing acceptance of euthanasia and assisted suicide in society.

As you read, consider the following questions:

1. According to Kopp, how many million patients receive hospice care annually in the United States?

2. How many Americans does the author report die annually under hospice care?

3. How many Americans are killed by stealth euthanasia every year while in hospice, according to the author's estimate?

When *Roe v. Wade* was decided in 1973, we were caught off guard. We had to build a pro-life infrastructure almost from scratch to provide alternatives for women with crisis pregnancies. We now find ourselves at a similar point with euthanasia. We know that stealth euthanasia is here, that it is essentially legally protected already, and its prevalence is going to explode. We need to warn and educate the public. We also must identify and network with pro-life health care providers who are striving to provide ethical end-of-life care within a health care system that is becoming increasingly comfortable with prematurely ending the lives of certain patients. We urgently need to build the pro-life infrastructure that is still missing, but which is essential to providing concrete alternatives to stealth euthanasia.

Taking Stock

As we swiftly move toward the close of 2013, with the full implementation of the Affordable Care Act (ACA) on the immediate horizon, it is prudent to take stock of where the pro-life movement stands.

Despite measures in the ACA which will undeniably increase the overall rates of abortion (with estimates that new abortion coverage under the ACA will result in taxpayers subsidizing up to 111,500 abortions each year[1]), the culture at large is becoming more pro-life. Abortion clinics are closing at record rates and health care providers have no interest in entering the abortion field. Gallup polls in 2012[2] revealed that Americans now self-identify as pro-life at record rates. The pro-abortion movement is horrified to see the graying of its own movement as America's youth reject the pro-abortion agenda and swell the ranks of the pro-life movement. On the issue of abortion, there is great reason for hope. Anyone attending the March for Life each year in Washington, DC, witnesses this heartening change.

Looking at the opposite end of the life spectrum, there is cause for grave concern.

In the USA, approximately 2.5 million people die annually from all causes. Approximately 1.7 million patients receive hospice care annually (with more than 200,000 discharged alive from hospice care each year). With each passing year, a higher percentage of total yearly mortality occurs within the context of hospice and palliative care.

The roots of hospice care are thoroughly Christian, based on the corporal and spiritual works of mercy and dating back a thousand years to the times of the Crusaders in the Holy Land. In the 20th century, hospice care was a continuation of the work of Irish and French nuns dedicated to the care of the sick and dying, and furthered by Mother Teresa of Calcutta's global efforts. Modern hospice care, with its interdisciplinary approach and modern methods of alleviating physical, emotional and spiritual suffering, was the brainchild of Dame Cicely Saunders, an Evangelical Christian who came to her faith in a study group founded by C.S. Lewis at Oxford University. When hospice care is provided by professionals who still strive to uphold these Godly roots, it can be an awesome resource for the patient and loved ones, with nothing to fear.

Unfortunately, the overall picture today does not reflect the roots of hospice philosophy. Of the 1.5 million who die annually under hospice care, a growing number are dying premature deaths due to "stealth euthanasia," primarily via overmedication, terminal sedation and withdrawal of hydration and nutrition. Furthermore, hospice Medicare fraud is soaring. Most of the large corporate hospice providers have been accused of millions, and in some cases billions, of dollars in insurance fraud, often certifying patients for hospice care who were not actually dying, while profit-driven negligence in patient care has hastened the deaths of many.

Because death records never list overmedication, terminal sedation, deliberate dehydration or neglect as the immediate cause of death, it is very difficult to obtain concrete data regarding the number of those dying in such circumstances. However, having spoken with pro-life leaders in the end-of-life care field, I think it is safe to say that the numbers are not small and that they are increasing rapidly. A very conservative estimate would be that about one out of five patients under the care of the hospice and palliative care industry are caused to die premature deaths at present. That is 300,000 deaths by stealth euthanasia yearly. Many in the hospice and palliative care field are trying to make terminal sedation the standard of care. Those who are terminally sedated cannot take food and water, and the end-of-life care industry rarely provides assisted nutrition and hydration. As terminal sedation becomes more prevalent, the number of those dying by euthanasia will increase steadily.

ObamaCare Rationing

Unfortunately, health care rationing is going to contribute to the increasing number of premature deaths in health care settings. The Independent Payment Advisory Board (IPAB), the "death panel" being instituted under the ACA that Sarah Palin warned us about, will be tasked with rationing health care spending and making life-and-death decisions for enrollees. During the 2008 presidential campaign, Obama telegraphed where health care rationing is heading when he said that the elderly needed to be encouraged to forgo expensive care in the last years of their lives, choosing instead palliative or hospice care. When directly questioned about refusing an elderly women who needed surgery, he responded, "Maybe this isn't going to help. Maybe you're better off not having the surgery, but taking the painkiller."

Those whose surgical procedures or expensive medical plans of care are deemed by the IPAB to be "futile" will be sent home or to the nursing home, hospice or palliative care unit to "take the painkiller."

Stealth euthanasia will become the norm. Most laws that directly prohibit physician-assisted suicide also protect physicians whose use of opioids, sedatives and antipsychotics for pain management or alleviation of agitation might also hasten death. Thus stealth euthanasia, under cover of law, is little different than the outright legalization of abortion through nine months of pregnancy that was the result of *Roe v. Wade*.

The pro-life movement is at a crossroads. As the total number of surgical abortions has dropped to approximately 1.1 million per year, the number of stealth euthanasia cases has rapidly increased. As the total percentage of those who die in the USA within the context of hospice and palliative care climbs and the cultural acceptance and general practice of stealth euthanasia increases, we could see deaths by euthanasia surpass deaths by abortion within a generation.

It is indeed urgent that we build the pro-life infrastructure necessary to provide ethical alternatives to euthanasia.

Notes

1. "Affordable Care Act Could Fund Over 100,000 Abortions," Christine Rousselle, Townhall.com, 9/26/2013.

2. "'Pro-Choice' Americans at Record-Low 41%," Lydia Saad, Gallup.com, 5/23/2012.

> *"Whether or not we are family, friends, or politicians, we don't have the right to delay our sense of loss so that people who are in pain continue to suffer."*

The Affordable Care Act Could Bring Attention to the Death with Dignity Movement

Roy Speckhardt

Roy Speckhardt is the executive director of the American Humanist Association. In the following viewpoint, he regards the Patient Protection and Affordable Care Act, commonly known as the Affordable Care Act (ACA) or Obamacare, as a major step in the fight to ensure that Americans have the essential health care services they need. Speckhardt maintains that despite an individual's belief on the issue of assisted death, it is not right to impose those beliefs on those struggling to make end-of-life decisions. As a humanist, he personally supports the right of those with terminal illness and unbearable pain to end their lives if they so choose, as long as there are safeguards such as a psychological evaluation to ensure that the patient is of sound mind. He hopes that the debate over the ACA will bring attention to the issues of euthanasia and assisted suicide and the role of the death with dignity movement as a component of modern health care.

As you read, consider the following questions:

1. According to the author, in what year did the American Humanist Association express its support for the right to die movement?

2. How did Anastasia Khoreva end her own life in March 2012, according to Speckhardt?

3. What does Speckhardt say is essential to remember about the foundation upon which the modern health care system is built?

As the recent media reports on the Supreme Court's examination of the constitutionality of the Patient Protection and Affordable Care Act (known by some as Obamacare), many Americans are contemplating the future of national health care policy. Now that our attention has been focused on this issue, it's important to discuss a controversial topic that usually gets swept under the rug in the conversation about health care.

While almost all of us agree that life is a beautiful experience full of wonder, struggle, love, and many more worthy experiences, we must also acknowledge that for some it may have become irreversibly painful and unwanted. For these people, the trauma associated with disease and the restrictive nature of age transforms continued living into a daily exercise of pain and humiliation. Our empathetic sense of compassion in such cases dictates that we allow for a release from such suffering.

Since 1959, long before the activism of Jack Kevorkian, the Hemlock Society, and similar organizations (today lead by Compassion & Choices), the American Humanist Association has firmly supported the right of those who face incurable suffering to end their lives if they so choose, as long as all possible safeguards against misuse of the law are provided. Like Oregon's Death with Dignity Act it makes sense to have medical and psychological personnel evaluate people to make sure efforts to alleviate suffering have been attempted, and that the individuals are of sound mind when making such an irreversible decision.

This thinking is based in part on the question regarding whether a human being truly "owns" his or her own life or if that life belongs to another (e.g, their family, their society, their god). Humanists conclude that every single human being is the ultimate owner of his or her body and mind. Therefore, a person has the right to end his or her own life, and it's up to society to make sure that right is maintained and it's not abused by those who might gain from the demise of others.

Consider the story of Anastasia Khoreva, a 105-year-old woman who survived the Russian Revolution and two world wars. Friends said the great-great-great-grandmother had been depressed after being stricken with a lung infection and had expressed a desire to commit suicide. Anastasia ended her life in March [2012] by hanging herself and was discovered by her loved ones shortly after. This case didn't have to end in the tragic way it did. What if, instead of violently killing herself alone in a room and traumatizing those who found her, Anastasia had been allowed to go to a hospital for an end-of-life procedure? What if her final moments had been in a bed, surrounded by her loving family and friends as she painlessly drifted into unconsciousness and then died?

Exercising true compassion in situations like this may mean understanding a loved one's desire to break out of the prison of life in which they experience constant torment. We, as outsiders, may feel that prison is more desirable to nonexistence, but we must recognize that this choice is not ours. Whether or not we are family, friends, or politicians, we don't have the right to delay our sense of loss so that people who are in pain continue to suffer. Nor do we have the right to impose our religious beliefs regarding assisted suicide on others.

The Patient Protection and Affordable Care Act is a beginning in the struggle to ensure that Americans are given the vital health care services they need to survive. But health care shouldn't just be focused on prolonging life. It should also work to improve the quality of life of patients and grant them a pain-free escape from suffering after the request is properly evaluated by trained professionals. It is essential to remember that the desire to help another human being is the foundation upon which the modern health care system is built, and in that effort we must recognize that occasionally the help that is desired is a compassionate ending of a life filled with anguish.

As the health care debate continues, this issue deserves special attention. People like Anastasia Khoreva and her family should not have to suffer the trauma of an undignified and painful death. A solution should be devised to ensure that those who no longer wish to live are able to go about ending their own lives in a dignified and safe way.

Periodical and Internet Sources Bibliography

The following articles have been selected to supplement the diverse views presented in this chapter.

Jamelle Bouie	"Obamacare Fear-Mongering Hall of Fame: Death Panels and More," Daily Beast, September 30, 2013.
Tanya Connor	"Legalizing Physician Assisted Suicide Still a Threat," *Catholic Free Press*, October 8, 2013.
Charles Hurt	"Sarah Palin Knew a Death Panel When She Saw One," *Washington Times*, November 5, 2013.
Aaron Klein	"More Evidence of 'Death Panels' in Obamacare," WND.com, January 5, 2013.
Sarah Kliff	"A Quarter of Head and Neck Surgeons Think Obamacare Has Death Panels," *Washington Post*, December 19, 2013.
Brian Koenig	"Oregon Expands 'Death Panel' Healthcare System," *New American*, August 15, 2013.
Dan K. Morhaim	"Affordable Care, Death Panels, and Personal Freedom," *Huffington Post*, July 17, 2012.
Kate Pickert	"The Health Care Proposal That Spawned the 'Death Panels' Lie Is Back," *Time*, July 25, 2013.
Wesley J. Smith	"Will Obamacare Boost Assisted Suicide?," *National Review Online*, October 3, 2013.
Peter Ubel	"Why It Is So Difficult to Kill the Death Panel Myth," *Forbes*, January 9, 2013.
Mary Elizabeth Williams	"The Opposite of 'Death Panels:' How the ACA Could Lead to a Better Way of Dying," Salon, October 2, 2013.

For Further Discussion

Chapter 1

1. Adam J. MacLeod compares palliative care and assisted suicide. What is MacLeod's main argument for supporting palliative care over assisted suicide? Do you agree or disagree with his argument, and why?

2. Peter Singer reviews the findings of a report on end-of-life decision making and argues that individuals should have the right to end their lives on their own terms. In your opinion, should individuals be granted this right? Why, or why not?

3. E.J. Dionne contends that people do not have any more right to kill themselves than they do to kill another person. He supports palliative care to comfort terminally ill patients. Do you think Dionne provides sufficient evidence to support his argument? Explain your answer.

Chapter 2

1. Terry Pratchett outlines his endorsement of assisted suicide and calls for a tribunal that would examine an individual's case for assisted death. Do you agree or disagree with Pratchett's suggested tribunal, and why?

2. According to Sherif Emil, euthanasia is a dangerous problem in Quebec. What reasons does Emil give for this conclusion? Do you agree with Emil's argument? Explain.

3. Steve Siebold believes that society should not allow religion to influence the assisted death debate. Based on the arguments in the viewpoint, do you agree with Siebold? Why, or why not? Explain.

Chapter 3

1. Luke J. Davies asserts that euthanasia for children should be permitted. Conversely, Charles Foster argues against child euthanasia. Which author offers the more compelling argument, and why? With which author do you tend to agree? Explain your reasoning.

2. Mary Elizabeth Williams claims that people faced with extreme emotional suffering should have the option of assisted death. In your opinion, should assisted death be permitted for those suffering from emotional pain? Provide reasons to support your answer.

3. As Chethan Sathya reports, most doctors throughout the world oppose physician-assisted suicide and euthanasia. What are the reasons for this universal opposition? Do you agree with the physicians' stance? Explain your reasoning.

Chapter 4

1. Adam Goldenberg argues that Canada's death panels offer an objective process for resolving end-of-life dilemmas. In your view, should the United States adopt similar death panels? Why, or why not? Explain.

2. Roy Speckhardt maintains that health care should provide a pain-free and dignified escape from suffering. Do you agree with Speckhardt that part of a compassionate health care system is allowing suffering patients to end their lives if they so choose? Explain your reasoning.

Organizations to Contact

The editors have compiled the following list of organizations concerned with the issues debated in this book. The descriptions are derived from materials provided by the organizations. All have publications or information available for interested readers. The list was compiled on the date of publication of the present volume; the information provided here may change. Be aware that many organizations take several weeks or longer to respond to inquiries, so allow as much time as possible.

American Life League
PO Box 1350, Stafford, VA 22555
(540) 659-4171 • fax: (540) 659-2586
website: www.all.org

The American Life League believes that human life is sacred. It works to educate Americans about the dangers of all forms of euthanasia and opposes legislative efforts that would legalize or increase its incidence. It publishes the bimonthly pro-life magazine *Celebrate Life*, and it distributes videos, brochures, and newsletters monitoring euthanasia-related developments. Its website offers links to articles such as "Obamacare Is to Euthanasia What 'Roe v. Wade' Was to Abortion," "Euthanasia: We Can Live Without It," and "A Deadly Conflict of Interest: Why Euthanasia in Belgium Is So Out of Control."

Caring Connections
1731 King Street, Alexandria, VA 22314
(800) 658-8898
e-mail: caringinfo@nhpco.org
website: www.caringinfo.org

Caring Connections, a program of the National Hospice and Palliative Care Organization (NHPCO), works to improve care at the end of life. It provides free resources and information to people making decisions about end-of-life care and services. Available at its website is information about end-of-life issues, grief, caring for loved ones, and understanding hospice and palliative care. Additionally on its website are brochures and articles such as "Conversations Before the Crisis: The Intersection of Family, Faith and Policy in Advance Care Planning."

Center for Bioethics and Human Dignity (CBHD)

Trinity International University, 2065 Half Day Road
Deerfield, IL   60015
(847) 317-8180
e-mail: info@cbhd.org
website: www.cbhd.org

The Center for Bioethics and Human Dignity (CBHD) is the Christian bioethics research center at Trinity International University. It provides news, information, and analysis on bioethics issues from a Christian perspective. Resources available at CBHD's website include reports, podcasts, and case studies such as "Clinical Ethics Dilemmas: Experiencing Differences Between European and American End-of-Life Care."

Death with Dignity National Center

520 SW Sixth Avenue, Suite 1220, Portland, OR   97204
(503) 228-4415 • fax: (503) 967-7064
e-mail: info@deathwithdignity.org
website: www.deathwithdignity.org

The Death with Dignity National Center is a nonprofit, nonpartisan organization. It serves to defend and promote death with dignity laws across the United States by providing information, education, research, and support for laws that allow terminally ill patients to end their own lives. The organization's website provides a blog, a research center that discusses death with dignity acts across the country, and articles such as "Bridging the Hospice Gap" and "So You Want to Pass a Death with Dignity Law in Your State."

Ethics and Public Policy Center (EPPC)

1730 M Street NW, Suite 910, Washington, DC   20036
(202) 682-1200 • fax: (202) 408-0632
e-mail: ethics@eppc.org
website: www.eppc.org

The Ethics and Public Policy Center (EPPC) is a Washington–based think tank that applies Judeo-Christian moral tradition to critical issues of public policy. The EPPC and its scholars work to promote America's founding principles, including respect for human dignity and individual freedom. It publishes the *New Atlantis*, a quarterly journal covering a variety of issues, including assisted suicide, with articles such as "In Whose Image Shall We Die?" and "Ten Years of 'Death with Dignity.'"

Ethics in Medicine

Department of Bioethics and Humanities, Box 357120
University of Washington School of Medicine
Seattle, WA   98195
(206) 543-5145 • fax: (206) 685-7515
e-mail: bioethx@u.washington.edu
website: depts.washington.edu/bioethx

Ethics in Medicine is an educational website of the University of Washington School of Medicine's Department of Bioethics and Humanities. The website maintains a comprehensive database of information relating to a wide variety of ethical issues, including physician aid in dying. It also includes a section on ethical tools that provides a clear overview of ethical principles and methodology in physician aid in dying. It provides discussion and case studies on physician-assisted suicide and end-of-life issues.

Euthanasia Research and Guidance Organization (ERGO)

24829 Norris Lane, Junction City, OR   97448-9559
(541) 998-1873
e-mail: ergo@efn.org
website: www.finalexit.org

The Euthanasia Research and Guidance Organization (ERGO) is a nonprofit organization that believes voluntary euthanasia, physician-assisted suicide, and self-deliverance are all appropriate life endings. Its mission is to provide information and literature on end-of-life care and assisted-suicide laws throughout the world. Available at the ERGO website are videos, books, and essays, including "The Case for Physician-Assisted Suicide and Voluntary Euthanasia."

Exit International

PO Box 4250, Bellingham, WA 98227
(360) 347-1810 • fax: (360) 844-1501
e-mail: contact@exitinternational.net
website: www.exitinternational.net

Exit International is a leading nonprofit euthanasia/assisted suicide information and advocacy organization. With offices in the United States, Australia, and England, the organization aims to provide accurate end-of-life information and pushes for the legalization of assisted suicide. Exit International publishes the *Deliverance* newsletter and the *Exit Internationalist* e-newsletter.

Hastings Center

21 Malcolm Gordon Road, Garrison, NY 10524
(845) 424-4040 • fax: (845) 424-4545
e-mail: mail@thehastingscenter.org
website: www.thehastingscenter.org

Founded in 1969, the Hastings Center is a nonprofit research institute that works to address fundamental ethical issues concerning health care, biotechnology, and the environment. The center conducts research and education as well as collaborates with policy makers to identify and analyze the ethical dimensions of their work. It publishes two periodicals—the *Hastings Center Report* and *IRB: Ethics & Human Research*—which provide articles such as "A Peaceful Death or a Risk to People with Disabilities?" and "A Suicide Right for the Mentally Ill? A Swiss Case Opens a New Debate."

Human Life International (HLI)
4 Family Life Lane, Front Royal, VA   22630
(800) 549-5433
website: www.hli.org

Human Life International (HLI) rejects euthanasia and believes assisted suicide is morally unacceptable. It defends the rights of the unborn, the disabled, and those threatened by euthanasia. It provides education, advocacy, and support services. HLI publishes the quarterly magazine *FrontLines* as well as online articles on euthanasia such as "Majority of Americans Find Suicide Immoral, but Split on Doctor-Assisted Suicide."

National Catholic Bioethics Center (NCBC)
6399 Drexel Road, Philadelphia, PA   19151
(215) 877-2660 • fax: (215) 877-2688
e-mail: info@ncbcenter.org
website: www.ncbcenter.org

Founded in 1972, the National Catholic Bioethics Center (NCBC) promotes and safeguards human dignity. NCBC strives to be a positive force in promoting the dignity of each person, from conception until natural death. Its website includes a frequently asked questions section as well as the full text of the Vatican's *Dignitas Personae* instruction concerning respect for human life. The organization also publishes a quarterly journal and provides publications such as "A Catholic Guide to End-of-Life Decisions."

Patients Rights Council
PO Box 760, Steubenville, OH   43952
(800) 958-5678
website: www.patientsrightscouncil.org

The Patients Rights Council is a nonprofit organization that addresses euthanasia, assisted suicide, and end-of-life issues from a public policy perspective. The organization networks with individuals and groups to influence policy and news coverage. Available at the Patients Rights Council website are numerous resources, including a table outlining the assisted-suicide laws in the United States and a frequently asked questions section about euthanasia and assisted suicide.

World Federation of Right to Die Societies

e-mail: robjonquiere@worldrtd.net
website: www.worldrtd.net/news

Founded in 1980, the World Federation of Right to Die Societies consists of fifty-three right to die organizations from twenty-six countries. The federation provides an international link for organizations working to secure or protect the rights of individuals to self-determination at the end of their lives. The federation believes individuals should be able to ask for assistance in dying if necessary. It publishes a biannual newsletter, and its website offers news updates and links to additional resources.

Bibliography of Books

Zakyah Basri — *Euthanasia: Which "M" Is It? Mercy or Murder?* Bloomington, IN: AuthorHouse, 2012.

Nan Bauer-Maglin and Donna Perry, eds. — *Final Acts: Death, Dying, and the Choices We Make.* New Brunswick, NJ: Rutgers University Press, 2010.

Katy Butler — *Knocking on Heaven's Door: The Path to a Better Way of Death.* New York: Scribner, 2013.

Lewis M. Cohen — *No Good Deed: A Story of Medicine, Murder Accusations, and the Debate over How We Die.* New York: HarperCollins, 2010.

Jeanne Fitzpatrick and Eileen M. Fitzpatrick — *A Better Way of Dying: How to Make the Best Choices at the End of Life.* New York: Penguin Books, 2010.

Elizabeth Price Foley — *The Law of Life and Death.* Cambridge, MA: Harvard University Press, 2011.

Stuart C. Goldberg — *Death with Dignity: Legalized Physician-Assisted Death in the United States 2011.* Seattle, WA: CreateSpace, 2011.

Neil M. Gorsuch — *The Future of Assisted Suicide and Euthanasia.* Princeton, NJ: Princeton University Press, 2009.

Derek Humphry *The Good Euthanasia Guide: Where, What, and Who in Choices in Dying.* Junction City, OR: Norris Lane Press, 2008.

Richard Huxtable *Euthanasia: All That Matters.* New York: McGraw-Hill, 2013.

Emily Jackson and John Keown *Debating Euthanasia.* Portland, OR: Hart Publishing, 2012.

Lynn Keegan and Carole Ann Drick *End of Life: Nursing Solutions for Death with Dignity.* New York: Springer Publishing Company, 2011.

Shai J. Lavi *The Modern Art of Dying: A History of Euthanasia in the United States.* Princeton, NJ: Princeton University Press, 2007.

Guenter Lewy *Assisted Death in Europe and America: Four Regimes and Their Lessons.* New York: Oxford University Press, 2011.

Michael Manning *Euthanasia and Physician-Assisted Suicide: Killing or Caring?* Mahwah, NJ: Paulist Press, 2014.

Philip Nitschke and Fiona Stewart *Killing Me Softly: Voluntary Euthanasia and the Road to the Peaceful Pill.* Waterford, MI: Exit International US, 2011.

Philip Nitschke and Fiona Stewart *The Peaceful Pill Handbook.* Waterford, MI: Exit International US, 2011.

Robert Orfali — *Death with Dignity: The Case for Legalizing Physician-Assisted Dying and Euthanasia.* Minneapolis, MN: Mill City Press, 2011.

Ron Panzer — *Stealth Euthanasia: Health Care Tyranny in America.* Rockford, MI: Hospice Patients Alliance Inc., 2011.

Craig Paterson — *Assisted Suicide and Euthanasia: A Natural Law Ethics Approach.* Burlington, VT: Ashgate, 2012.

Craig Paterson — *The Contribution of Natural Law Theory to Moral and Legal Debate Concerning Suicide, Assisted Suicide and Euthanasia.* Los Angeles, CA: Viewforth Press, 2010.

Alex Schadenberg — *Exposing Vulnerable People to Euthanasia and Assisted Suicide.* Port Huron, MI: Ross Lattner Educational Consultants, 2013.

Fran Smith — *Changing the Way We Die: Compassionate End-of-Life Care and the Hospice Movement.* Berkeley, CA: Viva, 2013.

Michael Stingl — *The Price of Compassion: Assisted Suicide and Euthanasia.* Buffalo, NY: Broadview Press, 2010.

L.W. Sumner — *Assisted Death: A Study in Ethics and Law.* New York: Oxford University Press, 2013.

Rodney Syme	*A Good Death: An Argument for Voluntary Euthanasia.* Carlton, Victoria, Australia: Melbourne University Press, 2008.
Stanley A. Terman, Ronald B. Miller, and Michael S. Evans	*The Best Way to Say Goodbye: A Legal Peaceful Choice at the End of Life.* Carlsbad, CA: Life Transitions Publications, 2007.
Sidney Wanzer and Joseph Glenmullen	*To Die Well: Your Right to Comfort, Calm, and Choice in the Last Days of Life.* Boston, MA: Da Capo Press, 2007.

Index

W

Y